QUICK COURSE

in

MICROSOFT®

INTERNET EXPLORER 5

ONLINE PRESS INC.

Microsoft Press

PUBLISHED BY
Microsoft Press
A Division of Microsoft Corporation
One Microsoft Way
Redmond, WA 98052-6399

Library of Congress Cataloging-in-Publication Data

Quick Course in Microsoft Internet Explorer 5 / Online Press Inc.
    p.   cm.
   ISBN 1-57231-989-5
   1. Microsoft Internet Explorer.   2. Internet (Computer network)
 3. World Wide Web (Information retrieval system)   I. Online Press
Inc.
 TK5105.883.M53Q54   1999
 005.7'13769 - - dc21   98-55332
                                 CIP

Printed and bound in the United States of America.

1 2 3 4 5 6 7 8 9   QMQM   4 3 2 1 0 9

Distributed in Canada by ITP Nelson, a division of Thomson Canada Limited.

A CIP catalogue record for this book is available from the British Library.

Microsoft Press books are available through booksellers and distributors worldwide. For further information about international editions, contact your local Microsoft Corporation office or contact Microsoft Press International directly at fax (425) 936-7329. Visit our Web site at mspress.microsoft.com.

A Quick Course® Education/Training Edition for this title is published by Online Press Inc. For information about supplementary workbooks, contact Online Press Inc. at 14320 NE 21st St., Suite 18, Bellevue, WA 98007, USA, 1-800-854-3344.

Authors: Joyce Cox, Ted Cox, and Eric Heydrick
Acquisitions Editor: Susanne M. Forderer
Project Editor: Anne Taussig

From the publisher

In today's busy world, everyone seems to be looking for easier methods, faster solutions, and shortcuts to success. That's why we decided to publish the Quick Course® series.

Why Choose A Quick Course®?

When all the computer books claim to be fast, easy, and complete, how can you be sure you're getting exactly the one that will do the job for you? You can depend on Quick Course® books because they give you:

- Everything you need to do useful work, in two easy-to-tackle parts: "Learning the Basics" (for beginning users) and "Building Proficiency" (for intermediate users).

- Easy-to-follow numbered instructions and thorough explanations.

- To-the-point directions for creating professional-looking documents that can be recycled and customized with your own data.

- Numerous screen shots to help you follow along when you're not at the computer.

- Handy pointers to key terms and tasks for quick lookup and review.

- Consistent quality—the same team of people creates them all. If you like one, you'll like the others!

We at Microsoft Press are proud of our reputation for producing quality products that meet the needs of our readers. We are confident that this Quick Course® book will live up to your expectations.

Jim Brown,
Publisher

Content overview

Content details

PART TWO   BUILDING PROFICIENCY

Introduction

This book is a fast-paced introduction to using Microsoft Internet Explorer 5. It is arranged in two parts. By the end of Part One, which consists of three chapters, you'll know enough about Internet Explorer to find the information you need and communicate with other Internet users. In the first chapter, we introduce the program, show you how to use the Active Desktop, talk a bit about intranets, and then take a look at the part of the Internet known as the World Wide Web. In Chapter 2, you take a tour of Internet Explorer's starting page, and you learn how to search for information and how to easily download files with FTP. In Chapter 3, we discuss communicating over the Internet with electronic mail (called *e-mail* from now on). Those of you who want more in-depth information will then want to move on to Part Two, which consists of three more chapters. In Chapter 4, we show you how to participate in newsgroups, where people with similar interests exchange information. Chapter 5 explores more Internet communication options with a variety of new tools that are part of Microsoft NetMeeting. Finally, in Chapter 6, you fine-tune your skills by learning how to customize Internet Explorer to suit your own taste.

The Internet is huge and far-reaching and its resources are so vast that it's easy to waste a lot of time if you don't know what you're doing. Instead of simply leading you from one nifty place to another, we show you techniques for using Internet Explorer to access Internet resources efficiently. (Of course, if you are paying for your own Internet account and you want to try your hand at "surfing the Net," feel free to explore all the interesting tangents you are bound to discover as you work your way through this book. Those of you who are taking this tour on someone else's nickel will want to check with the powers-that-be before using your work time for such surfing safaris, all the while running up hourly connect charges or monopolizing the resources of the computer that provides your access to the Internet.)

There's no such thing as free Internet access

People who access the Internet through corporate, government, or educational servers are often under the illusion that their Internet access is free. Although they may not have to pay for access out of their own pockets, *someone* is footing the bill for the computer resources and technology (fiber optic cable, satellites, and other communications gizmos) needed to make everything work. In the early days, Internet development was funded by government and public education agencies—in other words, by taxpayers like you and me. Now corporations and fee-paying users share the burden with these agencies, but the agencies still have to provide for Internet support in their tax-supported budgets.

What Do You Need to Use This Book?

We wrote this book using Internet Explorer 5 on computers running Microsoft Windows 98 and Microsoft Windows NT Workstation 4. We found only minor differences between them as far as Internet Explorer's operation is concerned. All our screen graphics are from Windows 98, but if you are running Windows NT you will have no difficulty following along.

We assume that the full version of Internet Explorer 5 is already installed on your computer and that you are ready to go. We don't cover all the ins and outs of choosing an Internet service provider (ISP) and configuring your system to make the necessary connections because many of you will have no choice about your avenue of access to the Internet. If you are using this book in conjunction with an instructor-led course, your instructor has already set up your learning environment using whatever Internet connection is available. Similarly, if you are using this book to teach yourself how to access the Internet from your computer at work, your supervisor or network administrator will already have set up your account and provided instructions for making the connection. If you want to access the Internet from your own computer, see the adjacent tip for hints about how to set up an Internet account.

Microsoft may issue upgrades to Internet Explorer from time to time, and the Web site you see when you start the program is updated frequently. What's more, the Internet itself is in a constant state of flux. So one thing you'll need as you work your way through this book is *flexibility*. For our examples, we have tried to select the more stable areas of the Internet, but even they are subject to change. So don't get uptight if your screen doesn't look exactly the same as ours. Change is a fact of life on the Internet, and staying flexible is the best way to cope with it.

The only other thing you'll need as you follow the instructions in this book is *common sense*. The growth in public interest in the Internet has been accompanied by a lot of media hype about the dangers of falling victim to a rip-off artist or a hacker, or of stumbling across unsavory information or unsavory characters. Let's put this hype in perspective.

Individual Internet access

One of the easiest ways to get hooked up to the Internet is to subscribe to an online service that provides Internet access, such as America Online (AOL) or The Microsoft Network (MSN). When you first click The Internet icon on your desktop, the Internet Connection Wizard may offer to help you connect using one of these services or to help you locate another Internet service provider (ISP). Alternatively, you can open an account with a local company that provides Internet access. To track down a local ISP, check advertisements in local newspapers. (A free weekly paper called *Computer User* is a good source if it is published in your area.) Before you sign on with any provider, check that you can use Internet Explorer 5 as your browser and ask for information about setting things up. Later on, if you are dissatisfied with your ISP and thinking of making a switch, you can check out the Web sites at *www.thelist.com* or *www.boardwatch.com* to find all the ISPs in your area.

How Safe is the Internet?

Well, it depends what you mean by *safe*. Usually people who ask this question have concerns that fall into one or more of the categories discussed below.

Information Security

The primary concern here is the confidentiality of personal and financial information, such as credit card numbers. When you send information across the Internet, it is routed from one computer to another depending on current traffic patterns until it reaches its final destination. Potentially, any computer along this unpredictable route can copy the information, and any criminally inclined person with access to that computer can then make use of it. Efforts are ongoing to create secure Web sites for buying and selling products and transferring confidential information, but it is up to you to exercise a little caution. Secure sites—those that encrypt information so that it cannot be hijacked in a readable form while it is in transit—are identified in Internet Explorer's status bar by a lock icon. If you don't see this icon, common sense says you shouldn't send out personal or financial information that you'd rather keep private. Internet Explorer provides a variety of features to help you protect both your wallet and your privacy and by default, displays a warning when you are about to send information to an unsecure site. See page 162 for more information about ways to protect against security leaks.

Credit cards

Secure sites

A secondary concern is the activities of programs known as *cookies*. When you visit some Web sites, the site transfers a tiny cookie file to your hard drive that collects information about your identity and about what you did when you visited the site. If you return later, the site checks the cookie file. Its information can then be used to tailor your current visit. However, the information could potentially be used to build a profile that would be valuable for targeted advertising. If you don't like the idea of this sort of information gathering, you can have Internet Explorer warn you when a cookie is about to be transferred to your computer or block the transfer entirely; see page 163 for more information.

Cookies

System Security

The concerns here fall into two categories: viruses and un-invited tampering. You can't "catch" a virus by looking at information on the Internet. But if you download an infected program and then run that program, you can end up with a very sick computer. Common sense says that if you want to acquire some of the goodies available on the Internet without becoming a victim of germ warfare, you should set up a system for checking your acquisitions before doing anything with them. Unfortunately, most people don't bother to set up such a system until *after* they are laid low by their first infection. Take it from someone who knows: viruses are not to be sneezed at. We urge you to invest in virus scanning software and follow the simple strategy on page 61 so that you can safely use the Internet's resources.

Another way to prevent rogue programs from damaging your computer is to take advantage of Internet Explorer's security features, which are designed to block programs from unknown sources, yet allow you to accept ones from trusted sources (see page 164). Until you have had a chance to investigate these features, our advice is to always abort any action for which Internet Explorer displays a warning message.

The concern about uninvited tampering stems from misunderstandings about *push* technology. Web browsing has traditionally been *pull* technology; nothing appeared on your screen unless you pulled it off the Web. With push technology, Web sites don't wait for you to come looking; they actively push their material at you. But here's the thing: they can't push anything in your direction unless you *ask* them to. We show you how on page 154, but in the meantime, you can rest easy.

Viruses →

Push and pull technologies →

Sleaze

Perhaps the most hyped-up danger of the Internet is that of coming face-to-face with the seedy side of life. There is no question that this possibility exists. However, in countless hours of working on the Internet, we have yet to experience this problem. On a few occasions where a sloppy search request produced listings that we could readily identify as sleaze, we simply avoided displaying the material. And we have deliberately steered clear of Web sites, e-mail messages, and newsgroups that we suspected might carry material we would find embarrassing or offensive. Common sense says that censoring the Internet not only flies in the face of the right to free speech but is also impossible given the Internet's global reach. Common sense also says that if you are concerned about sleaze on the Internet, you should use the filtering capabilities included in Internet Explorer or those of commercial filtering programs (such as CyberPatrol) to block the display of this type of information. On page 167, we show you how to use Internet Explorer's Content Advisor to prevent materials with specified language, nudity, sex, and violence ratings from being viewed on your computer.

Filtering capabilities

Sleazy People

Even with cookies and push technology, browsing the Internet is usually a one-way process. A Web site might count the number of people who visit it, but unless you fill out a questionnaire with personal information or allow cookies to be transferred to your computer, no one knows who you are. Sending e-mail and participating in newsgroups are two-way, interactive processes, and as with all interactions between human beings, they can bring you into contact with low-life characters you would ordinarily avoid. These people don't have your best interests at heart, and they may even want to do you harm. So common sense says that because you have no way of really knowing the people at the other end of e-mail messages or newsgroup articles, you should never divulge personal information such as address, phone number, or age. Internet Explorer can't help you with this one; it's up to you.

Like society in general, the Internet certainly has its criminal element, its red-light district, and its deviants. But as we've said, with a little common sense, you can take advantage of the huge positive part of the Internet without bumping into the very small negative part. It is that positive part that we'll explore in the following chapters. If you run into any security-related message boxes while you are exploring on your own, you will probably want to err on the side of caution and cancel the action that prompted the message until you've worked your way through this book.

CAUTION

LEARNING THE BASICS

In Part One, we cover the basic techniques for using Internet Explorer 5. After you complete these three chapters, you'll know enough about the Internet to be able to send e-mail and find information. In Chapter 1, you learn some Internet concepts, work with Internet Explorer's new interface, and take a short trip on the World Wide Web. In Chapter 2, you learn how to locate information on the Web and how to download files using FTP. Finally, in Chapter 3, you learn the ins and outs of e-mail using Outlook Express, which comes with Internet Explorer.

1

Introducing
Internet Explorer 5

We start with definitions of a few key terms, take a look
at the Internet Explorer 5 interface, and then fire up the
program for a quick jaunt on the World Wide Web. You
learn how to move around on the Web and what URLs
are all about.

This introduction to Internet Explorer 5 is ideal for new
users who are browsing the Internet for the first time, as
well as those who want a more thorough understanding
of Internet basics.

Tasks performed and concepts covered:

Use Web-style navigation buttons in My Computer

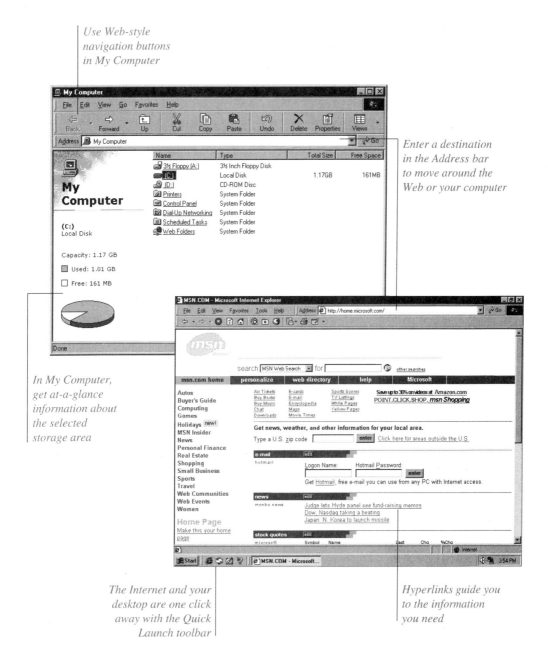

Enter a destination in the Address bar to move around the Web or your computer

In My Computer, get at-a-glance information about the selected storage area

The Internet and your desktop are one click away with the Quick Launch toolbar

Hyperlinks guide you to the information you need

Most books about the Internet assume you need a ton of background information before you can start exploring. Because we don't have to cover making connections and so forth, we can give you a few ounces of information and then jump right in.

Getting Oriented

In a few minutes, you'll fire up Internet Explorer, but we need to make sure we are all speaking the same language before you take the plunge. We promise to keep this short.

- **The Internet.** A contraction of *inter-networks* (or *between networks*). Started in the '60s as a connection between Department of Defense computers at four sites across the US, the Internet now connects millions of computers all over the world. Nobody "owns" the Internet, and nobody has overall management responsibility. Government agencies, universities, research establishments, and corporate entities own their particular network of computers and decide whether those computers will be connected to the Internet, who will be allowed to access them, and for what purpose. Anarchy is held at bay because the Internet is perceived as useful, and everyone cooperates to make it work. But other than broad rules governing connection technicalities and some even broader rules governing Internet behavior, everyone pretty much does his or her own thing. As a result, the Internet was used for years by only those experts who could navigate its maze of resources and deal with its mess of inconsistencies by typing cryptic commands.

- **Cyberspace.** Not a *thing*, but a *concept* first postulated by William Gibson in 1984 in his science-fiction novel *Neuromancer*. Cyberspace now refers to all the communication and other interaction that happens on the Internet. You can think of cyberspace as a global culture or society that is evolving its own language, customs, and other badges of membership.

- **The World Wide Web.** Invented by Tim Berners-Lee in 1989 in Switzerland, the Web is a special part of the Internet. Like the Internet, it's not a *thing*. It's a connection that allows people to view information stored on participating computers.

Internet II

The popularity of the Web has resulted in major connectivity problems for the agencies and institutions it was designed to assist. One possible solution to online congestion is being referred to as *Internet II*. Expected to take at least three years to put into place, Internet II is intended to serve scientists and scholars at research universities and high-tech companies. Whether this newer, faster service will ever be available to the general public remains to be decided.

The difference is that Web information is governed by a much tighter set of rules than information on the rest of the Internet. These rules specify how the text, graphics, and other elements should be formatted, so that information on one computer can be linked to information on another computer in a potentially infinite "web." The rules also mean that Web information is more consistent, making access to it easier for beginning and intermediate Internet users. For a lot of people, the Internet is the Web, because they never have any need or any desire to use the other Internet resources. As a result, these other resources are often relegated to the status of archives, while their updated versions are now published on the Web.

- **Web sites.** Information resources published on the Web by government agencies, companies, organizations, and individuals. Each site has an address called a *universal resource locator* (*URL*) that identifies the computer on which the files that make up the site's information are stored (see page 24). These files can consist of text, graphics, and multimedia components such as audio and video clips, all coded in such a way that they can be viewed by programs called *Web browsers* (see page 6). Web sites can also include mini-programs written in the Java language or using ActiveX controls (see the tip on page 35). Usually, the information stored at each Web site is divided into easily viewed chunks called *pages*, and the starting point of each Web site is its *home page*. You can jump from one page to another, both within a single Web site and between Web sites, by clicking *hyperlinks*, which appear on the screen as specially formatted text (usually a different color and underlined) or as graphics. (Don't worry if you're confused right now; all these terms will fall into place when you actually start moving around a Web site.)

← Universal resource locators (URLs)

← Web pages

← Hyperlinks

- **Internet service providers (ISPs).** Organizations that own the computers through which you access the Internet. Government agencies, educational institutions, and large corporations generally have computers that are directly connected to the Internet, and they control access for their individual members, students, or employees. The simplest way for small organizations and individuals to gain access is to use a modem to connect their computer to the computer of a commercial

Other types of resources

The most useful of the other resources available on the Internet include *FTP* (see page 61), *mail* (see page 66), and *news* (see page 96). Of declining importance are *Gopher*, *WAIS* (Wide Area Information System), and *telnet*, which we don't discuss in this book.

service that provides access for a fee. The term *Internet service provider* refers, in its narrowest sense, to this type of service and includes online information services such as The Microsoft Network (MSN) and America Online (AOL), as well as companies whose sole business is to provide access to the Internet. However, for simplicity we use the term *Internet service provider* in this book to refer to all avenues of access— whether you receive a bill or not.

- **Intranets.** Private Web look-alikes. Using Internet technology, many companies are setting up Internet servers and creating intranets that are accessible only from the company's computers (no matter where they are physically located). Intranets enable people to easily and cheaply access company information, exchange ideas, and collaborate on projects. A system of security "firewalls" ensures that intranet information is available only to the people in the company who are authorized to access it, not to general Internet users. (See page 15 for a brief discussion of intranets.)

- **Web browsers.** Programs you run on your computer so that you can view information stored on the World Wide Web. The browser interprets the information, displays it on the screen, and enables you to move between linked items. The first Web browsers, such as Mosaic, were developed on university campuses and were distributed for free. Since then, commercial companies have gotten in on the act, developing increasingly sophisticated browsers. As the browsers get fancier, so does the information available for viewing on the Web, to the point where high-ticket marketing companies are now in the business of designing Web sites that are as compelling as many television commercials. As you already know, this book is about the Microsoft Internet Explorer 5 Web browser.

That's it for the definitions for now. With that common understanding of what you're working with, let's turn our attention to Internet Explorer. In the next section, we assume you know how to start programs, give commands, work with tools such as dialog boxes, and otherwise manipulate objects in the Windows environment. If you don't, you might want to check out *Quick Course® in Microsoft Windows*, another book in our series, which will help you quickly come up to speed.

Extranets

Some companies are taking the concept of intranets one step further and are developing hybrid sites that allow outsiders, such as vendors and distributors, limited access to material stored on company intranets. Called *extranets*, these sites provide cost-effective, timely information to authorized people both inside and outside the company, while keeping the information secure from broader access.

Setting Up Your Working Environment

Before we give you a tour of Internet Explorer, we need to get everyone's computer settings in sync. Follow these steps:

1. If necessary, turn on your computer. After Windows starts, your desktop might look something like this:

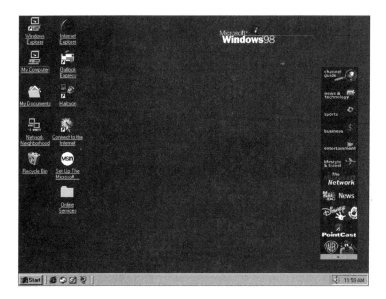

or it might look something like this:

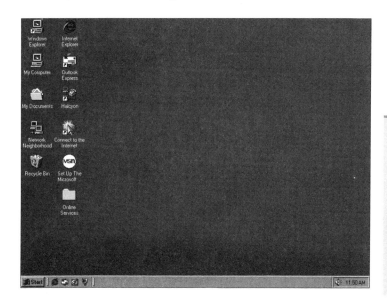

The Quick Launch toolbar

To the right of the Start button on the taskbar, you see the Quick Launch toolbar with buttons for quickly moving to the Internet. Also available for display on the Windows taskbar are the Address, Links, and Desktop toolbars; see page 160 for more information.

Why the difference? When Internet Explorer 5 is installed, it looks at your current Web browser configuration and carries over its settings. So if you upgraded from Internet Explorer 4 after implementing the Windows Desktop Update and turning on the Active Desktop, Internet Explorer 5 assumes you want to continue using your current configuration. You therefore see the first screen shown on the previous page. However, you may have upgraded from an earlier version of Internet Explorer (which did not have the Windows Desktop Update or Active Desktop); or from Internet Explorer 4 without the Windows Desktop Update implemented, or without Active Desktop turned on; or from a different browser; or from no browser. In any of these cases, Internet Explorer has no Active Desktop settings to carry over, and you see the second screen shown on the previous page.

Don't worry if the layout of your desktop looks different from ours. One of the hallmarks of Windows is the way you can set up your desktop to suit the way you work (or your company can set it up to suit the way it wants you to work). In the first column on the left of our desktop are the familiar icons for My Computer and Recycle Bin, as well as a shortcut icon for Windows Explorer. In the second column are icons pertaining to Internet communications. The shortcut to Halcyon is our Dial-Up Networking connection to our ISP. You may see an icon representing your avenue of access to the Internet, or access may be controlled by another computer on your network. The big *e* represents Internet Explorer (you're going to see this icon everywhere). The envelope icon represents Outlook Express, the e-mail service that comes with Internet Explorer. If you use a different e-mail program, you may see its icon on your desktop.

Different configurations

We wrote this book using a computer running Microsoft Windows 98 with the screen resolution set to 800X600. If you are using a different version of Windows or a different resolution, you might notice slight differences in the appearance of your screens. Don't be alarmed if your setup is different from ours. You will still be able to follow along with most of the examples in this book.

2. If you are using Windows 98, click the Start button, click Settings, and choose Folder Options. If you are using Windows 95 or Windows NT 4, open My Computer and then choose Options or Folder Options from My Computer's View menu. Either way, you see a dialog box something like the one shown on the facing page if you have the Active Desktop.

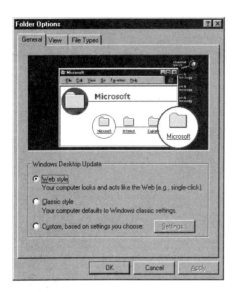

You see this dialog box if you don't have the Active Desktop:

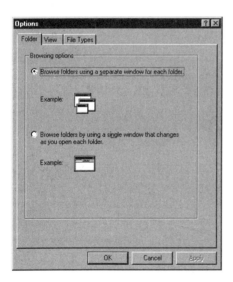

As you can see in the first dialog box, the Active Desktop users among you have three options when it comes to setting up your working environment:

- **Web style.** Implements all the features of the Active Desktop and revamps the Windows interface so that it can function like

What is the Active Desktop?

If you have the Active Desktop and are working in Web style, you can place items from Web pages directly on your desktop and, provided you are connected to the Internet, the items will be constantly updated from their source Web pages. See page 160 for more information about customizing your desktop with active Web items.

a Web page. This setting affects not only Internet Explorer but how you work with file-management tools such as My Computer and Windows Explorer.

- **Classic style.** Implements none of the features of the Active Desktop and leaves the Windows interface untouched.

- **Custom.** Allows you to determine which of the features of the Active Desktop you want to implement and which you would rather do without.

Non–Active Desktop users can select only how folders display their contents in My Computer.

3. If you can, click the Web Style option.

4. Whether or not you have been able to switch to the Web-style environment, click the View tab of the Folder Options or Options dialog box. Windows 98 users see these options:

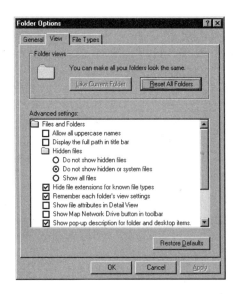

Initial capital letters

In this book, you'll notice that sometimes the option names we use don't exactly match those you see on the screen. We always capitalize the first letter of every word so that you won't stumble when you see the option names in a sentence. For example, in step 3, we tell you to click the Web Style option, when the option name on the screen is Web style. When all the words start with a capital letter, they stand out better, and we don't have to worry that our sentences will seem garbled.

Windows 95 and Windows NT 4 users see the options shown at the top of the facing page.

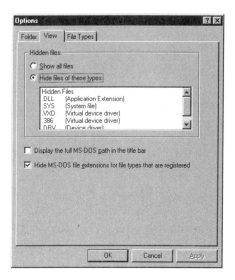

The options on this tab control which folders and files you can see when managing files, and such things as whether or not you see filename extensions.

5. If you are using Windows 98, click the Restore Defaults button and then click OK. Then click OK to use single-click if prompted.

Restoring the default view settings

6. If you are using Windows 95 or Windows NT 4, select the settings that match those in the dialog box shown above and click OK. Then close My Computer.

If you have switched to the Web-style environment, your screen now looks like the first screen shot on page 7. If you haven't, just read along for the next section or two, and then catch up with us on page 15, where we set the screen back to Classic style for the remainder of the book.

Trying Out Web Style

Let's see how the desktop behaves when it has a Web-like interface. To keep our commentary to a minimum, we'll avoid pointing out the obvious, but notice the subtle and not-so-subtle changes on the screen as you follow these steps:

1. Move the pointer over the Internet Explorer icon, noticing that the pointer changes to a hand and the icon's name changes

Pointing to select

color to indicate that it is selected, without you having to click it. This description pops up:

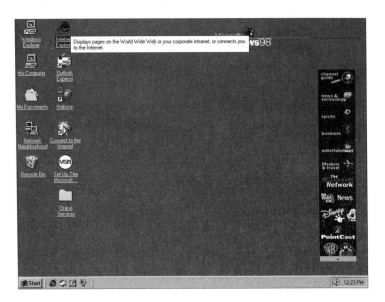

2. Point to each icon in turn to select it, but don't click anything.

3. Now click the My Computer icon once to open its window, which looks something like this:

Temporarily switching styles

You can switch the display style of a My Computer folder window without affecting any other windows. Choose As Web Page from the View menu to toggle this command on or off. If you toggle on the command when Classic style is active, you see the contents of the window in pseudo-Web style, but the icons aren't underlined; you click to select and double-click to open an icon. If you toggle off the command when Web style is active, you see the contents of the window in pseudo-Classic style, but the icons are underlined; you point to select and click to open an icon.

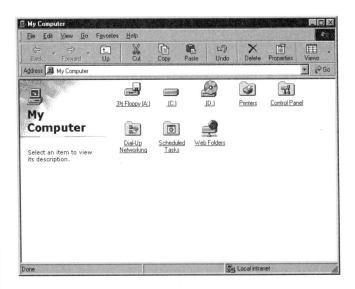

(If necessary, make the window about the same size as ours by dragging its borders.)

As you can see, with Web style, the information in the list box is presented in a different way.

4. Point to the (C:) icon in the My Computer window to select the drive. The window now looks like this:

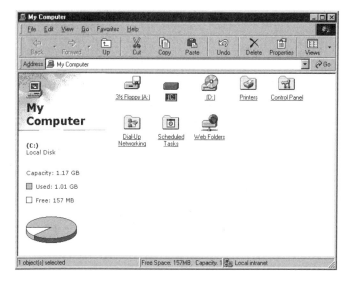

The Views button

5. Click the arrow to the right of the Views button on the toolbar and select Details from the drop-down list. If necessary, adjust the column widths to display all their information by dragging their header borders. Here's the result:

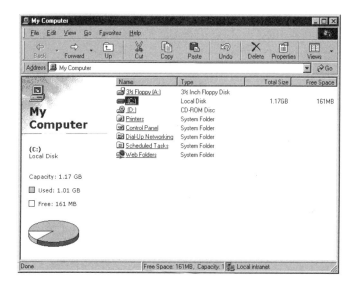

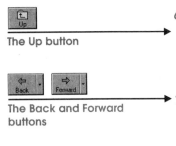

The Up button

The Back and Forward buttons

6. Click the (C:) icon to display its contents, and then click the Up button on the toolbar to move up one folder level to the My Computer window. Notice that changing the view in one window does not affect the view in other windows.

7. Next click the Back button to move to the previously displayed folder window. Notice that the Forward button is now active.

8. Experiment with using the buttons to move around, finishing up with the (C:) window displayed.

9. Click the Program Files folder icon to open its window, and then click the Internet Explorer folder icon.

10. Point to the first file icon in the second row to select it. Hold down the Shift key, move the pointer over to the third file icon in the row, release the Shift key, and then move the pointer to a blank area of the screen. All three files are now selected.

11. Now hold down the Ctrl key, point to the second file icon, release the Ctrl key, and move the pointer to a blank area. Here's the result:

Want the same view in all folder windows?

If you prefer a particular view, you can set that view as the default for all folder windows. (You can still change individual windows.) Choose Folder Options from the View menu, click the View tab, click the Like Current Folder button, and click OK. If you've changed the view for a few folders and you now want all of the folder windows to have the default view, select the Reset All Folders option in this dialog box.

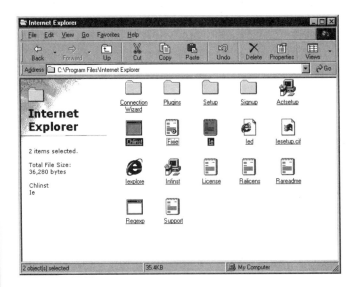

12. Click the arrow to the right of the Back button and select My Computer from the drop-down list, or click the Up button until you arrive at the My Computer window.

Once you have selected a file or folder, you can move, copy, or delete it in the usual way. However, you should perform these operations only with files and folders you have created, or you will almost certainly mess up your system.

Caution!

Reverting to Classic Style

After this little taste of Web style's impact on tools such as My Computer, let's get back on track so that you can get to know Internet Explorer. We've geared our instructions in this book to accommodate the broadest range of readers, and if you want to be able to follow along exactly with these instructions, you need to change your environment settings for the remaining chapters. (If you're used to Web style and don't want to change your configuration, you will still be able to follow along, but you may have to adjust the steps occasionally.) Follow these steps:

1. If you followed the instructions in the previous section, My Computer is open on your screen. If you simply read along, open My Computer now.

Changing styles

2. Choose Folder Options from the View menu to display the dialog box shown earlier on page 9.

3. Click the Classic Style option and then click OK.

4. Close My Computer and then open it again to confirm that you can now move around folder windows in traditional double-click fashion.

5. Close My Computer.

Accessing an Intranet

Companies and institutions are increasingly installing intranets to distribute information in a more efficient manner than is possible using paper. If your organization has an intranet, your system administrator may have created a configuration file that automatically sets up Internet Explorer on your computer to access the intranet. To implement the settings in this file, follow these steps:

1. Double-click the Internet Explorer icon on the desktop to start the program.

Other ways to start Internet Explorer

2. Choose Internet Options from the Tools menu and then click the Connections tab. Click the LAN Settings button. In the Automatic Configuration section, click Use Automatic Configuration Script and type the path of the file in the Address box. (Your system administrator will give you this information.) Then click OK twice.

Instead of starting Internet Explorer by double-clicking its icon on the desktop, you can click the Launch Internet Explorer Browser button on the Quick Launch toolbar. If you prefer the long route, you can also click the Start menu, select Programs, and then select Internet Explorer. To have Internet Explorer start automatically every time you turn on your computer, you can add an Internet Explorer shortcut to your StartUp menu. Right-click a blank area of the taskbar and then choose Properties from the shortcut menu. When the Taskbar Properties dialog box appears, click the Start Menu Programs tab, click the Add button to start the Create Shortcut Wizard, and click the Browse button in the wizard's first dialog box. Navigate to the Internet Explorer subfolder of the Program Files folder, double-click Iexplore, and then click Next. In the wizard's second dialog box, select the StartUp subfolder of the Programs folder and click Next. Click Finish in the wizard's last dialog box. Click OK to close the Taskbar Properties dialog box. The next time you start Windows, Internet Explorer will be ready and waiting for you.

From then on, your intranet's home page will automatically be loaded when you start Internet Explorer and you can apply the navigation techniques you learn in this chapter to your intranet's Web pages.

A Look at the Web

Quick Course books usually keep the amount of reading you have to do at any one time to a minimum and take a "learn by doing" approach to teaching software. We'll try to stick to that model as much as possible, but sometimes we can't avoid text explanations and still give you the information you need to understand the ins and outs of Internet Explorer. If you have an Internet account that limits the amount of time you can be online at a stretch, or if you live in a country that charges for telephone connection by the minute, you might want to take the time to read the text sections in each chapter before connecting to the Internet. Then when you're ready, you can join us for the step-by-step instructions.

Starting Internet Explorer

When you start Internet Explorer, you might be asked to enter an account name and password so that you can identify yourself to your ISP and gain access to the Internet. The exact procedure varies from provider to provider. In the steps on the facing page, we outline the procedure for accessing the Internet using a Dial-Up Networking connection to an ISP.

You should substitute the procedure for your own ISP or your network. Here goes:

1. Connect to your ISP.

The Internet Explorer icon

2. Double-click the Internet Explorer icon on your desktop to start the program. After some activity, Internet Explorer displays its starting page. Unless you are on an intranet, you probably see the MSN.COM home page provided by Microsoft.

3. If you see a page that asks what you would like to do first, click the underlined text that reads *Click here for a shortcut.* Your screen now looks something like this:

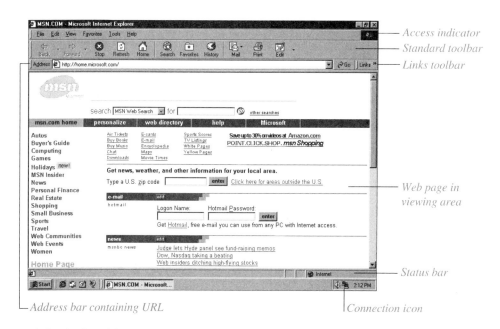

Access indicator
Standard toolbar
Links toolbar

Web page in viewing area

Status bar

Address bar containing URL

Connection icon

If displaying this page takes a while, don't be concerned. This site is accessed millions of times a day, and even with the fastest modem, access can be slow at peak traffic times.

No matter how big a monitor you have, with Web pages you never seem to have enough viewing space, so let's take a moment here to enlarge the viewing area a bit. Let's start by first turning off the labels on the Standard toolbar buttons and making the buttons smaller. (If you forget which button is which, you can always point to them and have ScreenTips display each button's name.) Follow the steps on the next page.

Customizing the toolbar

1. Choose Toolbars and then Customize from the View menu to display this dialog box:

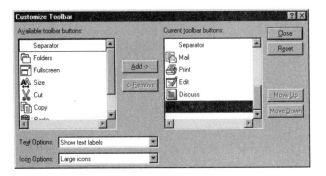

2. Change the Text Options setting to No Text Labels, change the Icon Options setting to Small Icons, and click Close.

At the left end of the menu bar, the Standard and Links toolbars, and the Address bar are *move handles* that you can use to rearrange these items to suit the way you work. Try this:

Move handles

Moving toolbars

1. Point to the Standard toolbar's move handle. When the pointer changes to a double-headed arrow, drag the toolbar up onto the menu bar and to the right until you can see all of the menus on the menu bar.

2. Now drag the Address bar's move handle until the bar sits to the right of the Standard toolbar. The Links toolbar, which was formerly lurking to the right of the Address bar, expands to take its place, like this:

More Buttons button

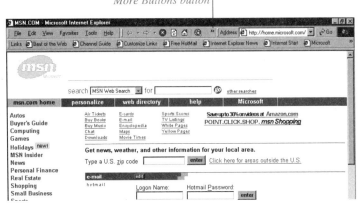

Adding and removing buttons

In the Customize Toolbar dialog box, you can edit the Standard toolbar. Select a button name in the Available Toolbar Buttons list and click Add; or select a button name in the Current Toolbar Buttons list and click Remove. You can change the order of buttons on the toolbar by clicking Move Up or Move Down.

3. What if you need to use a Standard toolbar button that's hidden? Click the More Buttons button at the right end of the Standard toolbar to drop down this palette of the hidden buttons:

The More Buttons button

4. Click a blank area of the window to hide the palette again.

Hiding a toolbar

5. Turn off the Links toolbar by right-clicking its name and choosing Links from the shortcut menu.

6. Next drag the Standard toolbar back to the toolbar row below the menu bar. Internet Explorer automatically resizes both the Address bar and the Standard toolbar.

7. To gain more viewing space, hide the Windows taskbar. Right-click a blank area of the bar, choose Properties from the shortcut menu, select the Auto Hide check box, click OK, and then click a blank area of the Internet Explorer window.

Hiding the Windows taskbar

Moving to Another Web Site

You'll come back to this Web page in Chapter 2 and use some of the tools it provides for navigating the Web, but for now let's take a look at the Quick Course Web site. (This is not a feeble attempt at self-promotion. Because Web sites come and go and change so often, sending you to our own site is the best way for us to know exactly what you are going to see as you move around. Once you are familiar with how Web sites work, we won't worry so much that you'll get disoriented if a site has changed since we wrote this book.) Follow these steps to move to a different site:

1. Click the URL in the Address bar to select it.

2. Now type *www,* then a period, then *quickcourse.com.* Check that the entire entry now reads *www.quickcourse.com* and press Enter. Internet Explorer adds *http://* in front of the URL, assuming that because you've typed a Web address, it should

More about the Address bar

As you'll see as you work your way through this book, the Address bar is a versatile component of the Internet Explorer interface. You can move it, size it, and use it to browse folders, run programs, and search the Internet.

use the HyperText Transfer Protocol to access the Internet resource you've specified. After a flurry of activity, you see this Quick Course home page:

Moving Around a Web Site

As you'll see, reading the information at a Web site is not at all like reading a book. Follow these steps to get a feel for how Web information is organized and how to move around a Web site:

Problems connecting to a Web site

If you see a message such as *The page cannot be displayed*, check to make sure that you haven't typed an extra period, misspelled a word, or otherwise entered the URL incorrectly. The message might also mean that the site's server is overloaded. Busy sites pose a common obstacle to Web connections. If you know that you've typed the URL correctly, you might want to try that site again later.

1. Move the pointer over the row of graphics below the title, noticing as you go that the pointer changes to a hand to indicate that the graphics are hyperlinks. (Don't click anything just yet.)

2. Scroll through the Quick Course home page using the scroll bar, and move the pointer over the text on the page, noticing how the pointer changes to a hand over underlined words to show that they are text hyperlinks.

3. Scroll to the top of the home page, point to the *Catalog* graphic hyperlink, and when the pointer changes to a hand, click the left mouse button. Your screen now looks like the one shown at the top of the facing page.

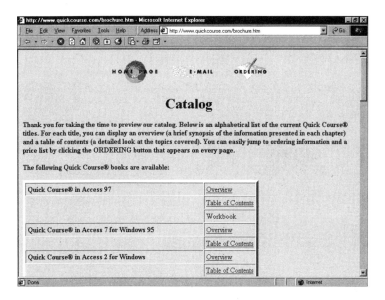

4. Next scroll the list of titles until you see *Quick Course in Windows 98*, and then click the Overview text hyperlink to display this page:

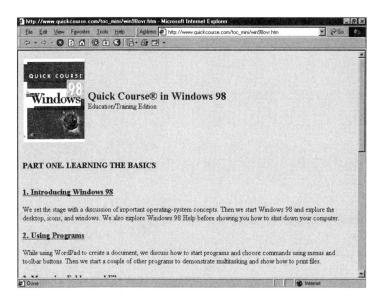

Suppose you want to go back to the title list to check out a different book. The Back and Forward buttons that you saw earlier on the My Computer toolbar also appear on Internet Explorer's toolbar, so you can move backward and forward through the pages you have already displayed, no matter which Web site those pages belong to. Try this:

Going back and forth

1. Click the Back button to redisplay the catalog page, then click Back again to redisplay the home page.

2. Click the Forward button to redisplay the catalog page. Notice that the Overview hyperlink for the *Quick Course in Windows 98* title has changed color to remind you that you have already viewed the information on that page.

3. Scroll through the catalog, clicking any *Overview* hyperlinks that interest you, and then return to the catalog page.

Some Web pages provide hyperlinks you can use to move directly from one part of the site to another. Check this out:

Jumping directly to the home page

1. Scroll to the top of the catalog page and click the *Home Page* graphic to move directly back to the Quick Course home page, the first page of this Web site. (Most well-designed sites include a hyperlink back to the home page from all the other pages in the site.)

2. Scroll the home page and click the *great comments* text hyperlink to display this page:

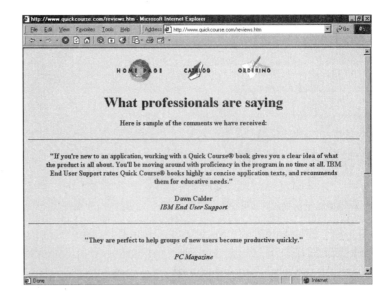

3. Click the Back button. (Clicking the *Reviews* graphic hyperlink at the top of the home page takes you to the same page as the *great comments* text hyperlink.)

4. Click the *frequently asked questions* hyperlink, and then click the second question, *Can you tell me something about Online Press?* This is what you see:

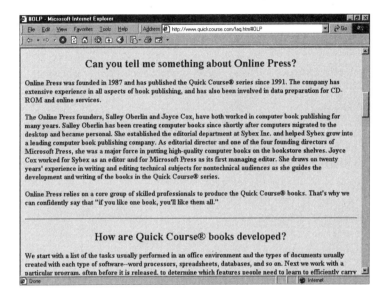

5. Click the Back button and then scroll the page. Notice that the page contains the list of questions at the top, followed by the answers. The hyperlinks you used previously all jumped to a linked file (a different page) that is stored at the same Web

Jumping to a different place on the same page

A few interesting sites

Here are URLs for a few other sites you might want to explore:

www.exploratorium.edu
The Exploratorium, a collection of news and resources related to science

www.intellicast.com/weather/usa
USA Weather, which gives the latest weather information for the United States

www.women.com
Women's Wire, which includes informative articles about women in business and entertainment

Frequently asked questions (FAQs)

So many Web sites include a frequently asked questions page that these pages have become known as *FAQs*. Clicking a hyperlink labeled FAQ takes you to a list of questions and answers, and this is a good place to start when you are looking for information on a Web site you haven't visited before.

site, whereas each question hyperlink jumps to a linked place within the same file (the same page).

6. Continue testing the hyperlinks at the Quick Course Web site until you can move around with ease, and then click the Home button on the toolbar to display Internet Explorer's starting page, shown earlier on page 17.

The Home button

7. If you have been collecting the addresses of Web sites you want to check out, enter one of them in the Address bar and explore another Web site now. (Remember, if you get lost, click the Home button to come back to familiar territory.)

Quitting Internet Explorer

When it's time to end an Internet session, the procedure you use will depend on your ISP. In our case, quitting Internet Explorer leaves us still connected to our ISP, so quitting the program and logging off our account are two separate procedures. In the following steps, substitute whatever procedure is appropriate for your setup:

1. Click the Close button at the right end of the Internet Explorer title bar (the X) to quit the program.

Temporarily displaying the
Windows taskbar

2. Point to the bottom of the screen to display the Windows taskbar. Then right-click the connection icon at the right end of the taskbar and choose Disconnect (or choose the command that signs you out of your Internet account).

Understanding URLs

You have just done a little exploring by entering the URL of a Web site in Internet Explorer's Address bar. Understanding how URLs are constructed can help you keep track of where you are on the Web and can also give you some insight into how Web pages are linked. Let's go over a bit of background information before you go online again.

As you can see on the facing page, this URL appears in the Address bar when you display the Quick Course Web site:

http://www.quickcourse.com

As we showed you, Web sites like this one are constructed of pages that are connected by hyperlinks. *Hypertext* files have text links, and *hypermedia* files have text links plus other types of links such as graphics, sound, and video links. (See the tip on page 32 for information about the origin of the term *hypertext*.)

You can jump from page to page because the people who publish Web information follow a set of rules called a *protocol*. The particular protocol used on the Web is the *HyperText Transfer Protocol* (or *HTTP*). So the first element of this URL tells Internet Explorer that you want to look at a Web resource. The resource is separated from the rest of the URL by a colon and two forward slashes.

The HTTP protocol

Next Internet Explorer needs to know the name of the computer, called the *server*, on which the Web resource is stored. This name, called the *domain name*, is a string of identifiers separated by periods. (If you have to say a domain name out loud, you call a period a *dot*, as in *www dot quickcourse dot com*.) The domain names of servers located in the US end in one of the following, which identify the type of domain:

The domain name

com	*Business organization*
edu	*Educational institution*
gov	*Government agency*
mil	*Military agency*
net	*Network administration support*
org	*Other type of organization*

(Because domain names are in increasingly short supply, the powers-that-be are trying to add new suffixes to this list.)

The domain name might also end in a two-letter code that identifies the country where the server lives.

When you clicked the *Catalog* hyperlink at the Quick Course Web site, you jumped to a page stored on the site's server as brochure.htm. As shown below, the URL in the Address bar changed to this:

http://www.quickcourse.com/brochure.htm

Paths in URLs

Here, the domain name is followed by a single forward slash and the *path* of the file specified by the hyperlink. The path tells precisely where on the server the file is located. In this case, the path is simply the name of the file, but it could also include folders and subfolders (directories and subdirectories), all separated by single forward slashes.

Why do you need to know all this? Can't you just click your way around using the simple techniques demonstrated earlier? Of course you can. But as you'll discover when you start searching the Web on your own, some Web sites are huge collections of files in which you can explore endless mazes of information. If you get lost or want to quickly retrace your footsteps without leaving the Web site, it's helpful if you have made a mental note of the site's key URLs so that you can quickly jump back to familiar pages. Let's put your new knowledge of URLs to the test:

1. Fire up your Internet connection.

The Launch Internet Explorer Browser button

2. Point to the bottom of the screen to display the Windows taskbar. Then start Internet Explorer by clicking the Launch Internet Explorer Browser button on the Quick Launch toolbar at the left end of the taskbar.

3. With Internet Explorer's starting page displayed on your screen, replace the URL in the Address bar with *www.city.net* and press Enter. Internet Explorer displays the Excite Travel page shown on the facing page.

Again, don't worry if this Web site has changed since we captured the screen pictured above.

4. Scroll down the page to the Find A Destination section, move the pointer over the *North America* hyperlink on the map, and click. Watch the status bar as Internet Explorer finds and opens this Web page, which is located at *http://www.city.net/regions/ north_america/?map*:

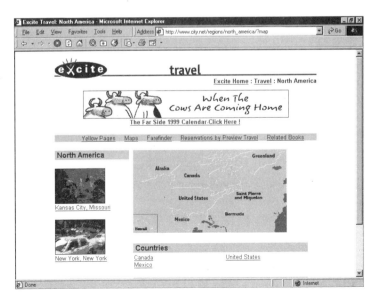

5. Point to the United States on the map of North America and click to display a map of the United States.

6. Click *Conn.* (for *Connecticut*) on the US map, and then click *New Haven* on the Connecticut map.

7. Suppose this line of investigation is not yielding the information you need. Click the URL in the Address bar to select it, press the End key to move the insertion point to the end of the URL, backspace to remove *connecticut/new_haven/,* and press Enter. Internet Explorer redisplays the map of the United States, and you can take another route through the site's information.

Let's look at a couple of other ways to jump back to a previously displayed Web page:

The History button

1. Click the History button on the toolbar to open the Explorer bar on the left side of the Internet Explorer window. The History list displays all the places you have visited today:

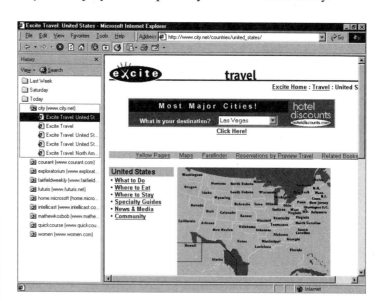

You can backtrack by selecting a site from this list, but don't click anything right now.

AutoComplete

If you begin to type the URL of a site you have already visited in the Address bar, Internet Explorer's AutoComplete feature drops down a list of URLs that match what you are typing. You can then either ignore the list and finish typing or select the URL you want from the list.

2. Click the History button to close the Explorer bar. Then click the arrow to the right of the Address bar to display a list of the sites you have visited:

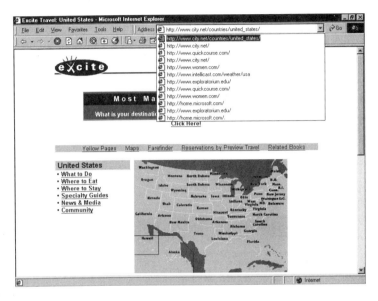

3. Choose *http://www.city.net/* from the list to jump directly to the Excite Travel page.

4. If you want, explore this Web site some more. Then quit Internet Explorer and disconnect from your ISP.

   Well, that's it for the quick tour. In the next chapter, we'll feature more ways of exploring the Web.

Finding Information
on the Web

You navigate around Internet Explorer's starting page, use a couple of Web search tools, and explore a reference Web site. You also learn how to return quickly to places you have already been, save pages for offline reading, and download files with FTP.

You can use the techniques learned in this chapter for locating any information on the Internet. Researchers and those working on extensive projects will find the ability to browse offline especially helpful.

Web pages visited and concepts covered:

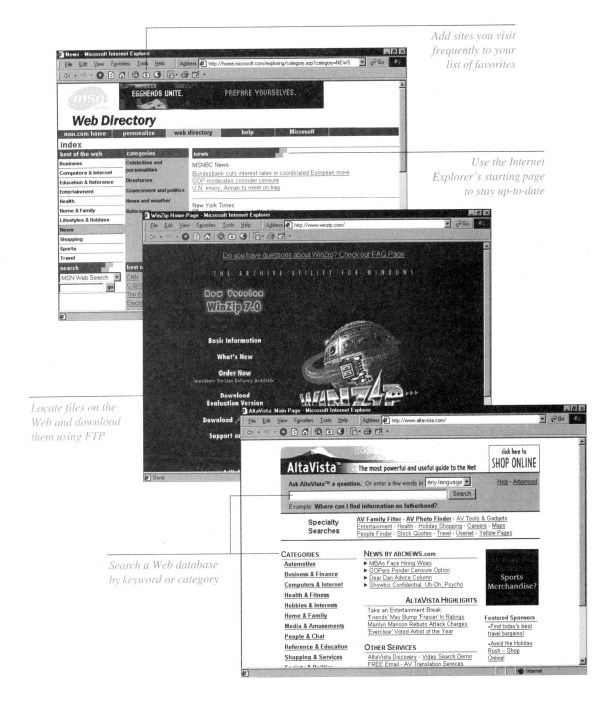

Add sites you visit frequently to your list of favorites

Use the Internet Explorer's starting page to stay up-to-date

Locate files on the Web and download them using FTP

Search a Web database by keyword or category

Until the early '90s, Internet activity was largely confined to government, academic, and research communities and was conducted in boring text formats. Commercial activity was not tolerated (see the tip on page 117). Although large areas of the Internet still operate this way, many users find no reason to explore them. Instead, they confine their activity to the World Wide Web, which not only presents its information in graphical formats that appeal to those of us reared on television and special effects, but also embraces capitalism by permitting advertising and online commerce. (It's worth noting that these characteristics go hand in hand. With the most elaborate Web sites costing millions of dollars to produce and maintain, it's not surprising that corporations at the forefront of Web creativity expect to be able to make a buck or two to justify their investment.)

In Chapter 1, you took a look at a couple of Web sites using Internet Explorer, and you learned the basics of navigating through cyberspace as well as some jargon. Whether you realize it or not, you already know enough to go *surfing*, meaning that you can jump among hyperlinked Web pages, checking out subjects that intrigue you and following topics from site to site across the world. But as appealing as it might be to spend hours exploring cyberspace, if you're like most people, you don't have time for open-ended wandering. Instead, you want to be able to tap into the Internet to find the answers to specific questions. Perhaps you need to track down an IRS form you need to complete your tax return. Maybe you've been asked to research a piece of equipment your company is considering buying, or you want to check the traffic patterns in your area to find the quickest route to a downtown meeting with a client. By the time you finish this chapter, you'll know how to use the various mechanisms provided by Internet Explorer and the Web to search for and retrieve the information you need.

Internet Explorer's Starting Page

Before you begin searching the Internet, you need to understand a bit about the various ways you can get at the information on the Web. With Internet Explorer, you seem to have a

The father of hypertext

The legendary Ted Nelson, a self-taught computer visionary, introduced the concept of hypertext in 1970 in his article "Barnum-Tronics," which was published in the Swarthmore College Alumni Bulletin. The following excerpt from that article was reprinted in his book *Computer Lib/Dream Machines* (1974).

"Hypertexts: new forms of writing, appearing on computer screens, that will branch or perform at the reader's command. A hypertext is a non-sequential piece of writing; only the computer display makes it practical. Somewhere between a book, a TV show and a penny arcade, the hypertext can be a vast tapestry of information, all in plain English (spiced with a few magic tricks on the screen), which the reader may attack and play for the things he wants, branching and jumping on the screen, using simple controls as if he were driving a car."

bewildering number of ways to access information, with lots of paths leading to the same places. As you know, when you open Internet Explorer, its starting page is displayed in the viewing area. This page has links to a diverse array of informational sites, including news, stock quotes, and sports. Rather than talking about them, let's jump right in and investigate a few. You can always come back later and explore the other links provided by this site. Here's how to get started:

1. Connect to your ISP and start Internet Explorer. While the program's starting page is downloading, notice that Internet Explorer displays a document icon and messages such as *Connecting to site* and *Opening page* at the left end of the status bar. To the right, a blue progress bar shows how much of the download process is complete. Meanwhile, a spinning icon at the right end of Internet Explorer's menu bar indicates that the program is busy accessing data and transferring it to your computer. When the word *Done* appears in the status bar, you see the starting page in the viewing area, like the one shown below:

The document icon

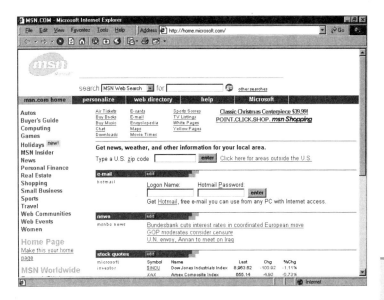

Your starting page will look different from this one because its information changes daily. However, the important navigational tools on the page should be the same as those you see

No status bar?

If you don't see the status bar at the bottom of the Internet Explorer window, you need to turn it on. Simply choose Status Bar from the View menu.

The hyperlinks bar

here, unless the page has been radically redesigned. (This happens frequently. Don't let it throw you off; a little sleuthing should be all you need to get oriented.) Toward the top of the page is a bar of hyperlinks that looks something like a menu bar. The hyperlinks represent the tasks you are most likely to want to perform and topics you can explore.

2. Click the *Web Directory* hyperlink to display a page that looks something like this one:

Notice that the same hyperlink bar appears again on this page.

3. Scroll the page, checking out its hyperlinks and the index on the left. (The hyperlinks on this page change frequently, so you will want to check the Web Directory often.)

4. Click the Home button on the Standard toolbar to return to the starting page.

5. Click the Back button on the toolbar to move back to the Web Directory.

As you have seen, you can access several categories of information from the Web Directory page. Depending on the type

What exactly is a hyperlink?

A hyperlink is a screen element containing embedded coding that specifies the address of the linked site. If you are interested in seeing the coding, simply choose Source from the View menu and scroll about. Hyperlinks are designated by a starting <a href = ...> code (the ellipsis is a placeholder for the linked address) and a closing </a> code. The information enclosed in these codes appears as a hyperlink on your screen.

of information you need, you might use this page as a starting point for a search, or as a way of staying up-to-date with the latest news on a variety of topics.

6. In the index on the left side of the page, click *News* to jump to this page:

The latest news

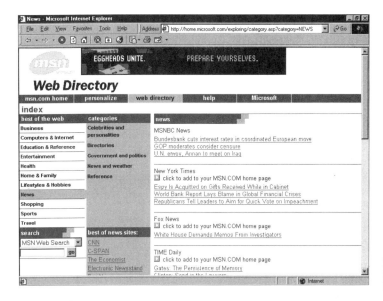

This page is divided into several sections, each containing separate blocks of information. The familiar hyperlink bar appears across the page and the index appears on the left. Also included are hyperlinks to categories of information and the news headlines. As you can see, the news comes from a variety of sources including MSNBC, the New York Times, and Time Magazine. You will learn later how to customize this page and add other news sources.

7. Scroll the news headlines, clicking various hyperlinks. Click the Back button on the toolbar each time to return to the News page so that you can take off in a different direction.

Suppose you want to stay up-to-date on news from the financial markets. Follow the steps on the next page to see how you might use Internet Explorer's starting page to accomplish this goal.

Java programs and ActiveX controls

As you surf the Web, you'll notice some sites include moving objects. These objects are rendered either by embedded *Java* programs or by *ActiveX controls*. Java is a programming language developed by Sun Microsystems. ActiveX controls are self-contained objects developed by Microsoft to perform specific types of functions. Both allow Web site developers to include animation and "moving" elements, such as scrolling words, in their pages. They also enable sites to interact with their visitors. To learn more about Java, check out the site at *http://java.sun.com*. To learn more about ActiveX controls, check www.microsoft.com/com/.

Financial information

1. Click the *Business* hyperlink in the index to display this page:

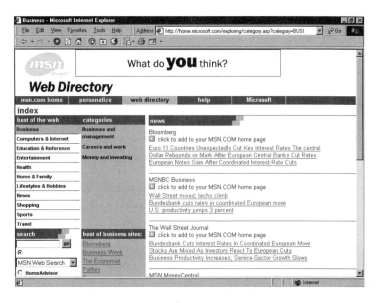

The links here include financial news, as well as links to management and career information.

2. Click various hyperlinks, noting any that provide the type of information you might want to look for later.

3. Click the Back button or use its drop-down list to return to the Web Directory page.

4. Check out other information categories, until you have an idea of the range of sources represented on the Web Directory page. In particular, you might want to look at the Travel category, where you can make travel-related reservations, and the Shopping category, where you can make purchases online. Notice that on all the category pages, a wide variety of resources and links is provided, making the Web Directory a particularly useful starting point for further exploration.

Travel information

Online shopping

Having seen how you might browse for current information on a variety of topics, as well as effortlessly spend money, let's move on to do some more specific research. In the next section, you'll learn how to gather information about a topic by using various Web search services.

Searching the Web

Suppose you work in the human resources department of a corporation and one of the company's managers has been recently promoted to director of the regional office in Boise, Idaho. The manager has asked you to research the real estate market in Boise and to see if Boise has a gym with a climbing wall. How would you use Internet Explorer and the Web to carry out this task?

You'll need to search a Web database—a collection of information about Web sites and their content. Several databases are available, but you'll look at just a couple of them. Because the techniques for searching are pretty similar for all the databases, you'll be able to check out the others on your own later.

Web databases are built using a variety of methods. Some rely totally on a program called a *Web crawler* that electronically works its way through the Web gathering information about the sites it finds; others use a Web crawler but also encourage Web site owners to submit information about their sites for inclusion in the database. (You might hear people talk about *worms*, *spiders*, and *robots*, which are types of crawlers.) Some databases are comprehensive and include everything; others focus on specific types of information. Some do little more than organize the information into categories; others add site reviews and ratings. Because of these differences, one database doesn't necessarily have the same information as another. The two databases you'll look at, Yahoo and Alta-Vista, are reputed to have the most powerful search engines.

◀ Web crawlers

◀ Worms, spiders, and robots

Searching by Category

To demonstrate searching by category, you'll use the Yahoo database, which began its life at Stanford University but has since graduated and become a commercial enterprise. In this example, you'll stick to researching Boise real estate, but you should check out Yahoo's features and capabilities on your own. To search for Boise real estate information, try this:

◀ Yahoo

1. If necessary, click the Home button to move to Internet Explorer's starting page. Then look at the top of the page, where you'll see edit boxes like those shown on the next page.

Accessing a search provider
from the starting page

In the first edit box, you specify the database, or *search provider*, you want to use by selecting it from a drop-down list. In the second edit box, you specify what you want to search for. Clicking Go initiates the search.

Accessing a search provider
from the Address bar

2. When you know the URL of the search provider you want to use, we've found that it's faster and more efficient to go directly to the service on the Web rather than going through the starting page. Click the Address bar, type *www.yahoo.com*, and press Enter to jump to the Web site shown here:

Searching for companies and people

Using Internet resources, you can easily look up names, addresses, e-mail addresses, and phone numbers. See page 92 for more information.

Why do security alerts keep popping up?

Throughout this chapter, you will see message boxes telling you that you are about to send information over the Internet that others might see. Because the information you are sending is not private or sensitive, you can simply click Yes to close the box. See page 162 for more information about zones and about Internet Explorer's other types of security.

3. Ignore the search box at the top of the page and instead scroll through the categories, noting their subcategories for future searches.

4. Under *Regional*, click *US States*. Then click *Idaho* in the list of states.

Regional information

5. On the Idaho page, click *Cities* in the Idaho Locations section. Then click *B* to move to the cities starting with that letter, click *Boise*, and click *Real Estate* on the Boise page.

6. Scroll the page and click *Boise Home Sites*. Internet Explorer jumps from Yahoo to the Web site maintained by The Idaho Statesman.

You can now retrieve examples of houses that are currently for sale in Boise by clicking the *Home Search* hyperlink.

Searching by Keyword

The alternative to searching a database by category is to search by keyword. You use a *search engine* that matches words you enter in a search box to words in a database. You could use Yahoo's search engine for this example, but instead you'll take another service for a spin. When it comes to searching by keyword, AltaVista is hard to beat. For this example, you'll enter the words *Boise* and *climbing gym* as keywords. Follow these steps:

AltaVista

1. As you did with Yahoo, go directly to AltaVista's Web site by typing *www.altavista.com* in the Address bar and then pressing Enter. (You can also click the Go button.) Internet Explorer displays the Web site shown at the top of the follow-ing page.

The Go button

When a search engine doesn't find a Web site

If you know that a Web site exists but the site doesn't show up in a search, it probably isn't included in the Alta-Vista database. The AltaVista Web crawler program starts with a core group of Web sites that have many links out into the Web, and it works its way from there, exploring all the linked sites and then their linked sites, and so on. As it goes, it checks old information and records new information in its database. If a Web site is not referenced by any link, the site's information won't make it into the AltaVista database, and the site won't show up in a search.

Using phrases as search
criteria

2. Click an insertion point in the edit box at the top of the page, type *Boise climbing gym*, and click the Search button.

3. Click Yes to confirm that you want to send this information over the Internet (see the tip on page 38). Then scroll the page to see results like these:

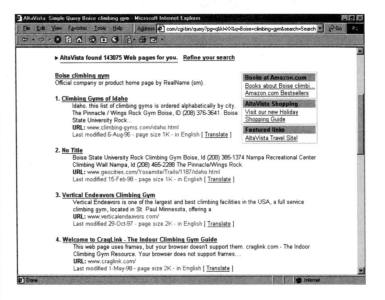

Unrelated Web sites

You may be puzzled by the re-sults of some searches, and some found sites may seem irrelevant. If you take the time to examine these sites, which are known as *false drops*, you will probably find one or more of the search terms you entered somewhere in the site's text. If the term is bur-ied, chances are the site isn't what you need, so it's best to focus on those sites whose relevance is obvious. Or the term might have more than one meaning, and your search terms weren't narrow enough to isolate the meaning you want.

Whoa! What happened here? How could all those Web sites contain the phrase *Boise climbing gym*? They don't; the sites contain *Boise* or *climbing* or *gym*—or any combination of those words. To get meaningful results from a Web search, you have to construct your search criteria very carefully to narrow down the results as much as possible. For a start, you don't want sites that contain the word *climbing* or the word *gym*; you want sites that contain the phrase *climbing gym*. We'll show you how to make this change with AltaVista. (Other search engines may have slightly different ways of defining search criteria. Check the service's Help feature to get the specifics for that engine.) Try this:

1. Scroll back to the top of the page, click an insertion point to the left of the *c* in *climbing* and type " (double quotation mark). Then add another quotation mark after the *m* in *gym* and click Search.

Narrowing your search

2. When Internet Explorer asks whether you want to turn on AutoComplete for Web forms, click Yes (see the tip below). Then take a look at the new results.

Well, that wasn't much help. Now you have a list of all the sites containing *Boise* or *climbing gym*. You need to narrow the search to those that contain both *Boise* and *climbing gym*. Here's how:

1. Click an insertion point to the left of the *B* in *Boise* and type + to specify that the matches must contain the following word. Then add a plus sign to the left of the first quotation mark and click Search. (To exclude a word, type a minus sign.) To see what a difference being specific makes, look at the results shown at the top of the next page.

Help from AutoComplete

If you often search for the same items, it makes sense to turn on Internet Explorer's AutoComplete feature so that you can pick the item from a list. If you click No when Internet Explorer asks whether you want to turn on Auto-Complete, you can turn it on later. Choose Internet Options from the Tools menu, click the Content tab, and then click AutoComplete. Next click the Forms check box in the Use AutoComplete For section and click OK twice. If your list gets too long to be useful, you can clear the record of AutoComplete entries in the AutoComplete Settings dialog box.

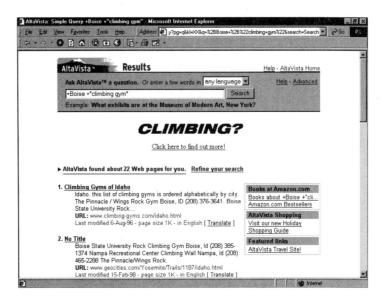

2. Now it is relatively easy to find the information you are looking for. Scroll the page to see the search results. Each of the listed Web sites starts with the site's title (if it has one) and the first few lines of the page. The entry also includes the Web site's URL, the date the Web site was last modified in AltaVista's database, the size of the linked file, and the language of the page. (There is a chance that older entries may no longer be valid; either the content may have changed or the site may have moved or disappeared altogether.)

3. Click the *United States Climbing Gym List* hyperlink to display a list of gyms categorized by state.

4. To quickly locate a gym in Boise, choose Find (On This Page) from the Edit menu to display this dialog box:

When Find doesn't work

Occasionally, the Find (On This Page) command won't find your Find What text. So why did the site show up in the web search results? Because you are looking in the AltaVista database of Web sites—not the sites themselves. Probably the site has changed since its information was added to AltaVista's database.

5. In the Find What edit box, type *Boise* and click Find Next. Internet Explorer searches the text of the displayed page and displays the first instance of *Boise* that it finds. Click Cancel

to close the dialog box, and scroll the page so that you can see the information shown here:

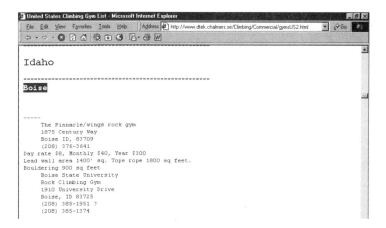

Mission accomplished! All you need to do now is copy the names and addresses, or you could print the information by following the instructions given on page 55.

Answering Specific Questions

We don't think the Internet will ever replace the dictionary or the phone book, but we can recommend it as a ready source of answers to several types of simple questions. For example, suppose you are sending a letter to Princeton, Missouri, and you don't know the zip code. You could get on the phone to the post office, but you can also find the answer on the Internet. The trick is to use a resource like Inter-Links, a Web site created and maintained by Rob Kabacoff. Try this:

1. With your Internet connection established and Internet Explorer running, type *http://alabanza.com/kabacoff/Inter-Links/* in the Address bar. (You have to type *http://* because the address doesn't start with *www*, and without one or the other, Internet Explorer has no way of knowing that the resource you want to work with is part of the Web.) Then press Enter to jump to the Web site shown on the following page.

Inter-Links

Advanced searches
In AltaVista, you can click the *Advanced* hyperlink at the top of the page and then enter more complex search criteria. You must use Boolean operators (AND, OR, NOT, or NEAR) between criteria in this type of search. You can also tell AltaVista to search a specific site element, such as the text or the title. Click the *Help* hyperlink to display more information.

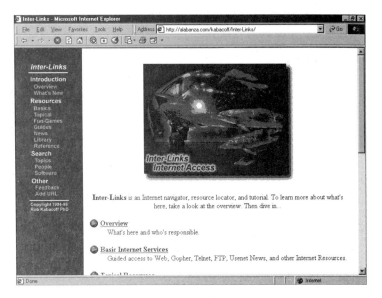

2. Scroll through the Inter-Links home page, which features hyperlinks to lists of more hyperlinks arranged by category. It's well worth exploring this site to get an idea of what kind of information is represented.

You're looking for the answer to your original question: what is the zip code for Princeton, Missouri? Follow these steps to see how to locate that information:

Checking a zip code ➤ 1. Click *Reference* under Resources in the index on the left, scroll the list of hyperlinks on the Reference Shelf page to get an idea of what's there, and then click *Zip Code Lookup*. Internet Explorer accesses a server at the United States Postal Service and displays the Web page shown at the top of the facing page.

About Inter-Links

The Inter-Links Web site is a free public service. It is Rob Kabacoff's "hobby"—meaning that it is not part of his job to maintain the site. As such, this site is typical of the many lists and directories created by Internet "old-timers," who believe that the free exchange of information is what the Internet is all about and who are willing to invest their own time in making information more accessible. You can find out more about Inter-Links by clicking the *Overview* hyperlink and then clicking the hyperlinks on the About Inter-Links page. You can also find out who Rob Kabacoff is by clicking his hyperlink. If you appreciate all the work he's done, you can drop him an e-mail message by returning to the Inter-Links home page and clicking the *Feedback* hyperlink.

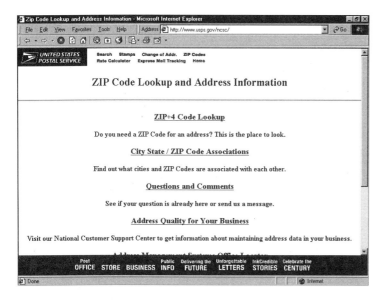

2. Click the *City State / ZIP Code Associations* hyperlink.

3. Next click the edit box, type *Princeton, MO*, and press Enter or click Process. The page now displays the zip code:

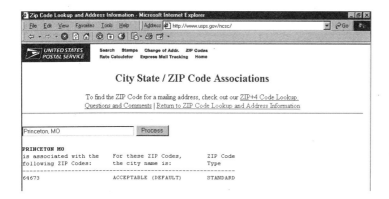

4. Search for any other zip codes you want to look up.

5. Click the arrow to the right of the Back button and select Reference Shelf from the drop-down list to return to the Reference Shelf page.

   Now suppose you want to set up a meeting with a client in a distant city in January of 2000. You are trying to figure out your flight plans so that you can take advantage of cheaper fares by staying over on Saturday night. Bring up an online calendar by following these steps:

Checking a date

1. Scroll to the bottom of the Reference Shelf list and then click *Perpetual Calendar* in the Other category. You see a calendar showing the current month.

2. In the month/year selector, change the date to January 2000 and click Jump. Here's the result:

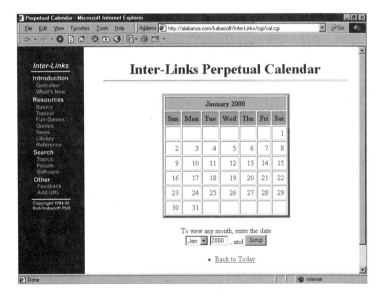

3. You might want to explore some of the other categories on the Reference Shelf page before you move on. By pointing to each category, you can see in the status bar whether the linked resource is part of Inter-Links or another Internet resource.

4. When you're done, return to the Inter-Links home page by clicking the Back button's arrow and then selecting Inter-Links, or by clicking the arrow to the right of the Address bar and selecting http://alabanza.com/kabacoff/Inter-Links/.

Now let's look at some of the other categories of information available from Inter-Links. Suppose you want to contact your US Senators to voice your opinion about a bill that is winding its way through the legislative process. Follow the steps on the facing page to find out how to reach them.

1. Click *Topical* under Resources in the Inter-Links index and then click *Government* under *Topics* on the Topical Resources page to display a list of hyperlinks to government resources.

Finding your senators

2. Click *Senate Homepage* under *Legislative Branch* to display this Senate Web site, which is located at *www.senate.gov/*:

3. Click the *Senators* hyperlink to display a list of hyperlinks to Senator information.

4. Click *Directory of Senators (by State)*, find your state, and click the name of one of your US Senators to move to his or her home page. For example, here's the page for Patty Murray, a US Senator from Washington State:

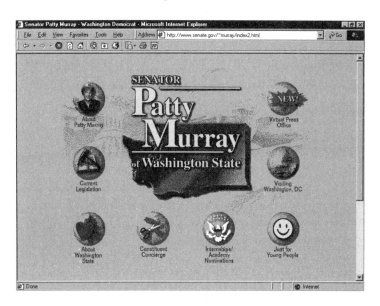

Other government and political sites

Here are some government agencies with Web sites and other political sites you might want to check out:

www.whitehouse.gov
The White House

www.usgs.gov
US Geological Survey

www.ed.gov
US Department of Education

www.odci.gov
The CIA

www.undp.org
United Nations Development Program

www.democrats.org
The Democratic National Committee

www.rnc.org
The Republican National Committee

Having found out how to contact your US Senators, you want
to check on the progress of the bill in question. Try this:

Finding legislative information

1. Redisplay the Inter-Links US Government page. (It's called
   Federal Government in the Back button's drop-down list.) Click
   Thomas: Legislative Information under *Legislative Branch* to
   display the Web site maintained by the library of the US Congress at *http://thomas.loc.gov/*:

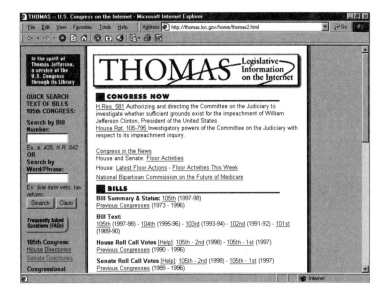

(If necessary, click *Thomas* on the announcement page to move
to this home page.)

2. Scroll through the Thomas home page to get an idea of the
   information you can access here, and then explore the *Bills*
   category, following the links of one specific bill.

3. When you've finished, make your way back to the Inter-Links
   US Government page and check out anything else that inter-
   ests you. For example, you might want to visit the Web site
   for the IRS (click *Federal Government - By Agency*, scroll to
   Department Of The Treasury, and then click *Internal Revenue
   Service*, or enter *www.irs.ustreas.gov/prod*). The IRS publishes
   The Digital Daily, a sophisticated online newsletter complete
   with animated graphics and scrolling text instructions. It takes

a while to download, but it's often worth the wait. You enter it by clicking the mailbox graphic on the IRS page.

4. Return to the Inter-Links home page and then click your way through any other features that interest you before moving on to the next section.

Returning Quickly to Sites You've Already Visited

You've looked at several Web sites in this chapter, some of which you may want to visit again in another session. It would be a pain to have to write down URLs whenever you find sites you want to return to, and with Internet Explorer, you don't have to. You can add a displayed page to your list of favorite places and have Internet Explorer remember the URL for you.

Using Favorites

Suppose you want to be able to access the Yahoo and Alta-Vista home pages without having to always enter their URLs. Follow these steps to add these two search services to your favorites list:

1. Type *www.y* in the Address bar. Then select www.yahoo.com from AutoComplete's drop-down list to display the Yahoo home page.

2. Choose Add To Favorites from the Favorites menu to display this dialog box:

3. You are given the opportunity to make the page available for offline browsing (see page 58), but for now just click OK to add the Yahoo page to your favorites list.

Turning off AutoComplete

If Internet Explorer's attempts to complete your entries in the Address bar bother you, you can just turn off the AutoComplete feature. Choose Internet Options from the Tools menu, click the Content tab, and then click AutoComplete. In the AutoComplete Settings dialog box, deselect Web Addresses in the Use AutoComplete For section, and then click OK twice.

4. Now display the AltaVista page using a different method. Click the History button on the toolbar to open the Explorer bar, as shown here:

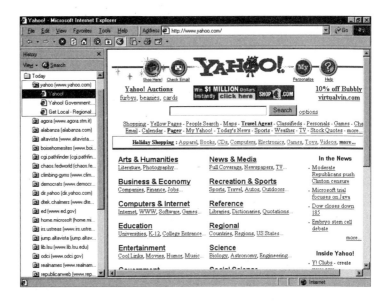

As you can see, the active Web site and all the pages you have visited at that site are outlined to make them stand out.

5. Click *altavista* to see a list of the pages you have visited at that site.

6. Click *AltaVista: Main Page* in the sublist, and then click the Explorer bar's Close button.

7. Now right-click a blank area of the AltaVista home page, choose Add To Favorites from the shortcut menu, and click OK to add the page.

8. Type *www.microsoft.com* in the Address bar and click the Go button to display Microsoft's Web site. Then repeat step 7, shortening the entry in the Name edit box to *Microsoft's Homepage*.

9. Now jump quickly to the Yahoo home page by choosing Yahoo! from the bottom of the Favorites menu.

Predefined favorites

The bottom half of the Favorites menu includes predefined entries arranged in folders, enabling you to reach the sites on the Channel bar and the Links toolbar, as well as various media sites, by choosing them from the menu. Also included is a Software Updates link that takes you directly to Web pages where you can find new versions of your programs.

10. Switch to AltaVista by choosing AltaVista Main Page from the Favorites menu.

Organizing Favorites

As you click your way around the Web, you will probably accumulate many favorites, and at some point, too many favorites will detract from your efficiency. Let's add a few more favorites to the list and then organize them into folders for easy retrieval. Follow these steps:

1. Add favorites for the following URLs by entering each one in the Address bar and choosing Add To Favorites from the Favorites menu:

   www.nytimes.com
   www.cnn.com
   http://update.wsj.com

   Notice that you need to subscribe to the Wall Street Journal to access all its many resources.

2. Choose Organize Favorites from the Favorites menu to display this dialog box:

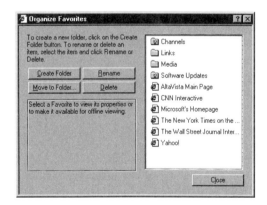

All your favorites are listed on the right side of the dialog box.

3. Click the Create Folder button, type *Daily News* as the folder name, and press Enter.

   <------------------------------
   Creating folders

4. Repeat step 3 to create a folder called *Search Tools*.

Moving favorites

5. Select AltaVista Main Page and drag it to the Search Tools folder. Then do the same with the Yahoo! favorite.

6. Next drag CNN Interactive and The Wall Street Journal Interactive Edition to the Daily News folder.

7. Click The New York Times On The Web favorite once to select it, and then click the Move To Folder button to display this dialog box:

8. Select Daily News as the destination folder and click OK.

Sorting Favorites

Whenever you add new favorites, it's a good idea to sort the list alphabetically. Obviously, sorting isn't crucial now, but it will become meaningful as your list expands. It's best to take care of this chore every time you add a new favorite. Here's how:

Moving folders in the list

1. In the Organize Favorites dialog box, click the Daily News folder to select it.

2. Drag the Daily News folder upward, releasing the mouse button when the black positioning bar is below the Channels folder.

3. Repeat this procedure to move the Search Tools folder below the Media folder. Then move Microsoft's Homepage to the top of the list.

4. Check the results of the sort and then close the Organize Favorites dialog box.

5. Now click the Favorites button on the toolbar to display your favorites list in the Explorer bar and see the effects of the new organization. As you can see, clicking Daily News displays a submenu like this one:

The Favorites button

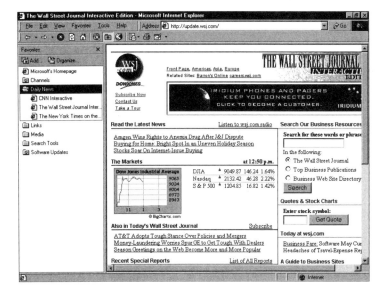

Deleting Favorites

Before leaving this discussion of favorites, let's delete the favorite for the Microsoft home page:

1. Click Organize on the Explorer bar to open the Organize Favorites dialog box.

2. Select Microsoft's Homepage, click the Delete button, and confirm the deletion.

3. Close the dialog box.

4. Next click the Favorites button on the toolbar to close the Explorer bar.

   The deleted favorite is now in the Recycle Bin. If you decide later that you want it after all, you can open the Recycle Bin and retrieve it. Otherwise, it will be deleted completely when the Recycle Bin is emptied.

Creating Desktop Shortcuts

Suppose you want to be able to keep up with the latest work of NASA (the National Aeronautics and Space Administration). You can create a shortcut to this agency's site on the Windows desktop and then simply double-click the shortcut to both start Internet Explorer and jump to that Web site. Here's how:

The NASA site

1. Type *www.nasa.gov* in the Address bar and press Enter to move to NASA's home page.

2. While you're here, take a minute to look around this really impressive site. It's great—and you paid for it!

3. For additional practice, add this page to your Favorites list.

4. Click the *today@nasa.gov* hyperlink to display this page:

5. To create the shortcut, right-click a blank area of the page and choose Create Shortcut from the shortcut menu. Internet Explorer displays this dialog box, asking you to confirm that you want a shortcut for this page to be created on your desktop:

6. Click OK to confirm the shortcut and close the dialog box.

Now let's test the new shortcut:

1. Close Internet Explorer by clicking its Close button, but don't disconnect from the Internet. On your desktop, you can now see a Web page shortcut icon.

2. Double-click the Today@nasa.gov shortcut icon. Internet Explorer automatically starts and takes you to the page.

The Web Page icon

Saving Information for Later Use

Sometimes you will find a Web page that is full of information you need, but plowing through it all online will take time (and perhaps consume too large a chunk of your Internet access budget). Or perhaps you come across a non-copyrighted graphic you would like to use. Or maybe you need to download an update for one of your programs. Here, we discuss ways to get information off the Internet so that you can use it at your convenience.

Printing Pages

The simplest way of saving Web information to read later is to print it. Clicking the Print button on the toolbar prints the current Web page directly to your printer. If the printer can handle graphics, they are printed along with the text. The process isn't foolproof. Not all printers handle Web printing well, and some page elements drop out no matter what printer you use. But under ideal conditions, what you get on paper is a pretty accurate rendition of what you see on the screen.

The Print button

Printing Selected Text

If all you want is part of the information on a Web page, you can streamline the printing process by printing a selection. This procedure not only saves printing resources, it can also save you a lot of time, especially if the page in question takes up multiple screens. Here are the steps:

1. With the Today@nasa.gov page still displayed on your screen, select the title and the first paragraph of the first article on the page by dragging across it, as shown on the next page.

Other ways to make Web content available

Desktop shortcuts are a familiar way to provide instant access to programs and information. On page 160, we discuss other ways to put the Web pages you use most frequently on the desktop so that they are never more than a mouse-click away.

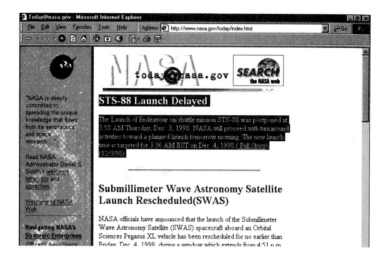

Your selection won't be the same as ours because the articles at this site change every day, but you get the idea.

2. Choose Print from the File menu to display this dialog box:

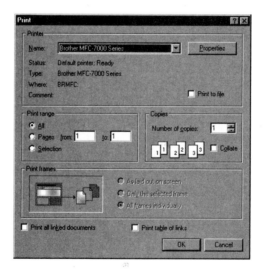

Notice the Print Frames section, which is currently unavailable, and the Print All Linked Documents and Print Table Of Links check boxes.

3. Click Selection in the Print Range section to tell Internet Explorer to print only the selected text, and then click OK.

Printing Frames

Some Web browsers, including Internet Explorer, can display Web pages that have been organized into sections called *frames*. Each frame displays its own file and acts independently of the other frames on the page. Not only can you view frames with Internet Explorer, but you can also print them in a variety of ways. Here's a demonstration:

1. Take a look at the Today@nasa.gov page and notice that there is only one scroll bar on the right side. Then scroll around and notice that although the page appears to be divided into two frames, in fact the entire page scrolls as a unit.

2. Click the Home button to return to the starting page and then repeat the experiment in step 1 with both the home page and the Web Directory page.

3. Now type *www.bookstore.washington.edu* in the Address bar and press Enter to open this page:

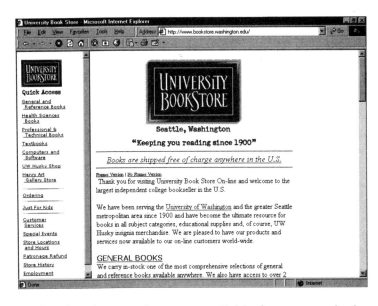

4. Notice that the page has two scrollable frames: one is the Quick Access list of contents, and the other is information linked to the list of contents.

5. Right-click a blank area of the Quick Access frame and choose Print from the shortcut menu. The Print dialog box opens with the Print Frames section now available.

6. Check that Only The Selected Frame is selected and click OK. Internet Explorer prints the Quick Access frame but not the other information on the University Bookstore page.

Frames are likely to become more common as more people upgrade to browsers that can handle them, so the ability to selectively print frames will come in handy in the future.

Saving Pages

The main advantage of printing pages is that you can read them anywhere. The main disadvantage—apart from using up paper—is that you have to remember where you put the printed pages if you need them later. If you save the pages as files on your hard disk, however, you can read their information on the computer but offline. (As you'll see in a minute, loading a page from disk can be much faster than accessing it on the Web.) One thing to take into account when saving Web pages is that they can hog a lot of disk space. If all you want is to be able to find the information later, it's more efficient to use favorites and shortcuts. With that in mind, let's create a Web Pages folder and save a couple of Web pages in it. For the first example, you'll save a page from the World Wide Web Consortium (W3C) that provides background information about the Web. Follow these steps:

HTML

The World Wide Web is made possible by *HyperText Markup Language* (HTML). It is enhanced by other coding systems such as Virtual Reality Markup Language (VRML) and by interactive ActiveX and Java components. When you save a file from a Web site, you are given the option of saving it either as an HTML file or as a plain text file. If you select Web Page Complete or Web Page HTML Only as the Save As Type setting in the Save As dialog box, the file is saved with its HTML coding so that it can be viewed offline in a Web browser. If you select Text File, the file is stripped of its coding and can no longer be viewed in a browser. You can, however, open it in a word processing program and view it there without formatting.

1. Type *www.w3.org/People/* in the Address bar, press Enter, and scroll to the section about Tim Berners-Lee, the inventor of the Web. Click his hyperlink, click *Press interviews*, and then click *my press FAQ* to open the page you want to save for offline reading.

2. Scroll through the page. Reading through all this material would take quite a while, so you'll save it as a file that you can read later.

3. Choose Save As from the File menu to display the dialog box shown on the facing page.

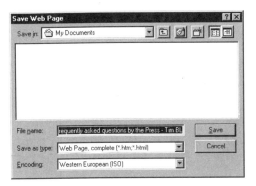

4. Click the Create New Folder button, name your new folder *Web Pages*, and open it.

5. Now type *Tim Berners-Lee* as the filename, leave the Save As Type option set to Web Page, leave Encoding set to Western European, and click the Save button. Internet Explorer saves the displayed page as a file.

Here's how to read the saved page offline:

1. Without quitting Internet Explorer, disconnect from your ISP. You can easily do this by choosing Work Offline from the File menu and then right-clicking your modem connection at the right end of the Windows taskbar and choosing Disconnect. (If your Internet configuration does not allow you to do this, end this session completely and then double-click the Internet Explorer icon on your desktop to restart Internet Explorer, clicking Work Offline if you are asked to reconnect to your ISP.)

Working offline

Saving only the text

Leaving the Save As Type option set to Web Page, Complete tells Internet Explorer to save all the files needed to display the page, including graphics, frames, and any other elements. If you want to save the text of the current Web page without the supporting elements, change the Save As Type option to Web Page, HTML Only. The resulting file can be viewed in a browser or edited with an HTML editor. You can also save the text of the page without HTML coding by changing the Save As Type option to Text File. If you just want to save an image of the page without the option of editing it, you can save it as a Web Archive file, which you can then e-mail to someone else.

Saving linked pages

Suppose you are viewing a Web site with a hyperlink to a page you want to read offline. To save the page without displaying it, right-click the link and choose Save Target As from the shortcut menu. (Choose Save Picture As for graphic links.) Name the file and then display and read it as usual.

Opening an HTML file 2. Choose Open from Internet Explorer's File menu to display the dialog box shown here:

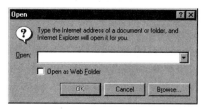

3. Click Browse to display the Browse dialog box, navigate to the Web Pages folder where the Tim Berners-Lee file is stored and double-click the filename to return to the Open dialog box with the name entered in the edit box. Then click OK. In a flash, Internet Explorer loads the page from disk.

4. If you want, you can now read this document in its entirety, without the overhead of being online.

Saving Graphics

You can find graphics of almost anything you can think of on the Web. Not all of it is great art—after all, most of it is free. But often a quick trip to the Web will yield exactly what you need to dress up a newsletter or a presentation. Here's the procedure for saving graphics on your computer:

1. Reactivate your Internet connection and Internet Explorer, and if necessary, choose Work Offline from the File menu to toggle it off.

Searching for graphics 2. On the Internet Explorer starting page, select MSN Web Search from the Search drop-down list, type *clip art* in the *For* edit box, and click Go.

3. On the Web Search page, scroll through the list of the first 20 sites that match your entry and then click one that offers free clip art.

4. If necessary, click other hyperlinks at the site until you find a graphic you'd like to save.

5. Right-click the graphic and choose Save Picture As from the shortcut menu. Internet Explorer displays the Save Picture dialog box, which is similar to the Save As dialog box.

6. If necessary, navigate to the folder where you want to save the graphic, name it, and click Save. Internet Explorer then saves the graphic file in *gif* or *jpeg* (or *jpg*) format (see the tip below), depending on the format of the original file.

You can now insert the graphic file in a document in the usual way.

Downloading Files with FTP

So far, you've explored only the part of the Internet known as the World Wide Web, but the Internet includes several other resources that have been around for a long time and are still actively used by Internet veterans who are less concerned with the hype and glitz of the Web than with easy access to information and tools stored on physically remote computers. One of these resources is the *File Transfer Protocol*, or *FTP*.

◄ The File Transfer Protocol

FTP is used for transferring files rather than for viewing them. In the old days, FTP was somewhat clunky and operated in an old-fashioned, text-only manner. Many computer systems all over the world store files that are available for downloading by any Internet user. Each remote system is set up to display a list of its downloadable files and to allow you to copy a selected file to your computer. However, many of these stashes of files can be accessed only in the traditional way. We won't worry about these files here, because the files you are most likely to want to copy to your computer are available for downloading in a much easier, more intuitive way using browsers like Internet Explorer, which have a built-in FTP program.

Why would you want to download a file? Often, new users start exploring FTP when they discover that a new version, bug fix, or enhancement is available for one of their programs. For example, Microsoft frequently announces the availability of downloadable upgrades for its products through its Web

Graphic formats

The Graphics Interchange Format (GIF) and Joint Photographic Experts Group (JPEG or JPG) formats are commonly used in Web pages because most Web browsers can display them. They also have the advantage of being compressed to save transmission time and storage space.

site. In the case of these programs, Internet Explorer takes you by means of hyperlinks to the file you need, and you may not realize you are using FTP to download the file. (When you download a file, you copy it from a remote computer—one that is not physically accessible—to your computer. You can reverse the operation and upload a file by copying it from your computer to a remote computer, but because you are unlikely to need to upload files, we don't cover uploading here.)

Scanning for viruses →

Caution. When you download a file, you should always store it in a temporary folder and scan the folder for viruses before you do anything with the file. You can't "catch" a virus by just looking at a file, but activating a file infected with a virus can wreak havoc. Although viruses usually do their damage via program files, new breeds of viruses attack word processor and spreadsheet files. So get in the habit of scanning *all* downloaded files with a virus program unless you are sure the files are coming from an impeccable source. Your chances of catching a virus are not great, but recovering from a virus is time-consuming and stressful. It is definitely worth taking a couple of minutes of your time to give all downloaded files a quick check.

In your travels around the Web, you may have come across sites that announced the availability of files for downloading. Often the name of the file is simply dressed up as a hyperlink,

Can you use it?

Two categories of text and graphics files and three categories of programs are available for downloading on the Internet. Text and graphics files can be:

- In the public domain, meaning that you can freely use them any way you want.
- Copyrighted, meaning that you can use them only if you have the copyright owner's permission and you state that the work is copyrighted and by whom. (There are some "fair use" exceptions.)

Programs can be:

- In the public domain.
- Freeware, meaning that you can freely use the program but, because the program's developer retains copyright to the software, you can't sell it.
- Shareware, meaning that you can use the program for a limited trial period. If you continue to use it, you should register and pay for it. Shareware is an honor system that has produced some great, low-cost programs, and we urge you to keep the programs coming by supporting their developers.

and clicking the link initiates the transfer process. For those of you who have erred on the side of caution and not yet taken advantage of one of these offers, we'll run through the steps for downloading a file from a Web site. For example, suppose you have received a compressed file with the extension .zip from a colleague. You know that you need the WinZip share-ware program to "unzip" the file (see the tip below). To locate and download the program, follow these steps:

1. Click the Home button. When Internet Explorer's starting page appears, enter *winzip* in the For edit box and then click the Go button.

Searching for programs

2. On the results page, click one of the *Winzip* hyperlinks to move to the site located at *www.winzip.com*, which looks something like this:

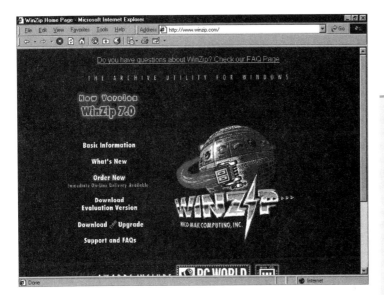

3. Click the hyperlink for downloading the evaluation version of WinZip and follow the links for your geographic location. Internet Explorer displays the dialog box shown at the top of the next page.

Compressed files

The last letters of a compressed file's name often tell you what program you need to decompress the file, as follows:

arc, arj	WinZip
hqx (Mac)	BinHex
gz	WinZip
lha	WinZip
sit (Mac)	Stuffit
tar	WinZip
z	WinZip
zip	WinZip

By the way, *gif* and *jpeg* graphics files are compressed files, but you don't need to decompress them to use them because they are auto-matically decompressed every time you display them.

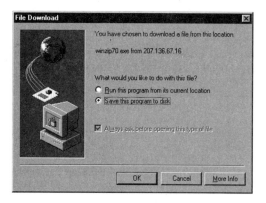

4. With the Save This Program To Disk option selected, click OK to display the Save As dialog box. Then navigate to the My Documents folder.

5. If you have not already created a folder in which to store downloaded files, click the Create New Folder button, type *Download* as the name of the folder, and press Enter.

6. Open the Download folder and click the Save button to store a copy of the selected file in that folder. Internet Explorer then displays a dialog box in which it reports its progress and estimates how it will take to download the file. This estimate is a function of both the speed of your modem and the volume of traffic on the FTP server. If you can't wait the estimated time, you can click Cancel and simply try again later when the server is not quite so busy. When Internet Explorer has finished downloading the file, you see a Download Complete message.

7. Click Close to close the message box.

Shareware.com

Shareware programs such as WinZip are often available from the Shareware.com Web site. It's worth checking this site for the programs you need before resorting to other search methods.

It's all done with mirrors

Popular FTP servers (and popular Web sites) often *mirror* their contents to other computers to provide distributed access to their information. The mirror server stores an exact copy of the parent server. The advantage to the user of this system is faster access; the advantage to the participating servers is reduced duplication of effort and a reduction in the amount of traffic on any one server.

8. If necessary, close Internet Explorer and disconnect from your ISP.

That concludes the demonstration of FTP. Before you do anything with the file you've downloaded, you need to scan the contents of the Download folder for viruses. You can then install WinZip by choosing Run from the Start menu, entering the path for the program in the Run edit box, clicking OK, and following the instructions on the screen. The program will then be ready to decompress any .zip files you receive.

Communicating
with Other Internet Users

Using Outlook Express, you learn how to send, reply to, and forward messages. You also learn how to use the Address Book, attach files, organize messages, and find e-mail addresses. The chapter ends with a discussion of online etiquette and e-mail conventions.

The techniques and procedures covered in this chapter will benefit anyone who wants to communicate with e-mail, whether for business or personal use.

Tasks performed and concepts covered:

Create folders to organize messages for easy retrieval

Attach files to messages for transmitting to one or more recipients

Receive both internal and Internet e-mail in one Inbox

Compose messages offline and send them to the Outbox for later delivery

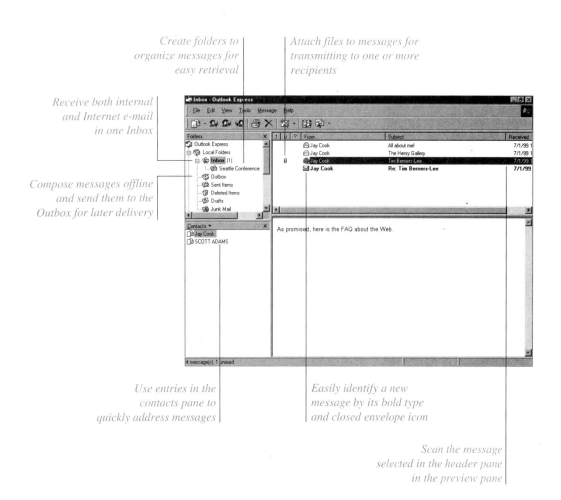

Use entries in the contacts pane to quickly address messages

Easily identify a new message by its bold type and closed envelope icon

Scan the message selected in the header pane in the preview pane

S o far, you have focused on the World Wide Web, which is primarily a means of publishing and obtaining information. Although Web sites are becoming more and more interactive, the majority are still passive, one-way channels of communication. This chapter discusses using Outlook Express for direct, two-way communication with other Internet users.

There's nothing difficult about the concept of e-mail. It's simply a way of sending messages that bypasses the traditional post office. The beauty of e-mail is that it doesn't use paper resources, it's fast, and it costs nothing (at least, nothing more than you are already paying for Internet access). Sometimes it is even better than using the phone because it enables you to deal with important business right away rather than run the risk of playing telephone tag. Additional advantages include the ability to attach files and programs to your messages and the fact that you can send the same message to several people without any additional effort. It's easy to understand why even people with abysmal letter-writing habits have become staunch advocates of e-mail as a means of communication. Using e-mail, you can fire off a note to someone living on the other side of the world or share your thoughts and ideas with politicians, company presidents, research scientists, and celebrities. (Of course, there's no guarantee that the recipients of your messages will actually read them, let alone respond to them!)

Like any other "good" thing, it's possible to have too much e-mail. Used wisely, e-mail can increase efficiency and reduce the amount of paper you use, but without a little restraint, e-mail can add unnecessarily to the burden of information overload. For example, if you get in the habit of sending messages to your entire department, everyone will feel obliged to spend time reading your messages whether or not they actually need to. Bear in mind this potential for misuse as you begin integrating e-mail into your daily routine.

Inappropriate, if not illegal, uses of e-mail

Just as there are inappropriate, and even illegal, uses of traditional mail services, there are also inappropriate uses of e-mail. Harassing or fraudulent e-mail is just as illegal as harassing or fraudulent regular mail. Mass e-mailing (junk e-mail, also called *spam*) and chain e-mailing are definitely frowned on by the Internet community. With regular junk mail, the receiver can decide at a glance whether to spend time and energy opening it. But with junk e-mail, the receiver is forced to spend both time and resources (connect charges and hard drive space) before he or she can make that decision. Because of this intrusion, junk e-mails are sometimes punished vigilante-style. The messages have been globally erased using programs called *cancelbots*, and the hard drives of their senders have been swamped by replies that have huge-but-useless file attachments.

Internet E-Mail Concepts

Sometimes people confuse internal e-mail with Internet e-mail, and it's easy to see why because in many ways, they are similar. However, having internal e-mail doesn't necessarily mean you have Internet e-mail. To be able to send e-mail to a colleague down the hall via internal e-mail, both your computer and your colleague's computer need to be connected to your organization's network. To be able to send e-mail to a customer in another state via the Internet, both your computer and your customer's computer need to be able to access the Internet.

As an example, suppose you want to use Outlook Express to drop a note to a customer thanking her for a recent order. You open Outlook Express's New Message window, enter the customer's e-mail address in the To box, enter a topic in the Subject box, type the message, and click the Send button on the toolbar. Outlook Express then adds information such as your e-mail address and sends the message from your computer to your ISP's *mail server*, which in turn sends it to the computer designated as the customer's mail server. That mail server holds the message in the customer's *mailbox* until she connects to the server, at which time her e-mail program downloads the message to her hard drive. She can then read and reply to it at her convenience. The reply makes the same journey in reverse. From the customer's computer, it travels first to her mail server and then to your mail server, which holds the reply in your mailbox. When you connect to your server, Outlook Express downloads the reply to your hard drive.

How e-mail works

Obviously, for such a seemingly simple process to succeed as well as it does, some pretty complex things have to happen behind the scenes. A lot of the work rests on the shoulders of two e-mail protocols called *Simple Mail Transfer Protocol* (*SMTP*) and *Post Office Protocol 3* (*POP3*), which control the way messages travel between your computer and your ISP's mail server, and between that server and other servers on the Internet. But for the most part, none of that concerns you. Once e-mail is set up on your computer, your main responsibility is getting people's Internet e-mail addresses correct.

E-mail protocols

E-Mail Addresses

E-mail addresses are like postal addresses, but instead of providing five or six items of information to send a letter, you need to provide only a couple of items to send an e-mail. A typical e-mail address might be *jdoe@mailserve.tld*. (If you had to say this e-mail address out loud, you'd say *jay doe at mailserve dot tee el dee*.)

The user name ──────────▶

The domain name ──────────▶

The part of the address to the left of the @ sign is a *user name*, which identifies the addressee. The part to the right of the @ sign is a *domain name*, which identifies the mail server where the addressee's mailbox is located. In our example, *jdoe* is the user name and *mailserve.tld* is the domain name. (In this example, the last part of the domain name—*.tld*, which stands for *top level domain*—is bogus. As with URLs, the last part of a real domain name—such as *.com*—identifies the type of domain; see page 25.)

In the universe of e-mail, many users can have the name *jdoe* and many users can have mailboxes at *mailserve.tld*. But only one user named *jdoe* can have a mailbox at *mailserve.tld*. In other words, *jdoe@mailserve.tld* must be a unique address. If a user named Joe Doe wants a mailbox at *mailserve.tld* and *jdoe* already exists, he must either choose a name like *joedoe* so that his e-mail address is *joedoe@mailserve.tld*; or he must move his mailbox to a different mail server so that his e-mail address is something like *jdoe@mailnet.tld*.

Obviously, to send e-mail to someone, you must know the correct e-mail address. (See page 92 for information about how to track down e-mail addresses.) If you send a note inviting Joe Doe to lunch but address it to *jdoe@mailserve.tld* instead of *joedoe@mailserve.tld*, who knows who might show up! More importantly, you might send critical, time-sensitive information off into cyberspace and never know why you didn't get a reply. (If an e-mail is sent to a nonexistent address, as opposed to the wrong person's address, it usually "bounces back," the equivalent of a return-to-sender stamp from the postal service.) The moral: double-check the address of the person you want to correspond with before you send a message on its way.

Setting Up E-Mail

If you work for a large organization or you access the Internet through a school computer, e-mail has probably already been set up on your computer. If that is the case, you can skip this section and jump to page 73, where we tell you how to start Outlook Express. If e-mail is not yet set up on your computer, you can't send or receive e-mail until you tell Outlook Express your name, the names of the servers that will handle your incoming and outgoing messages, your account name, and your password. As you'll see if you follow these steps, setting up Outlook Express is easy:

1. Obtain the domain names of your outgoing e-mail server and incoming e-mail server from your ISP.

2. Without connecting to the Internet, double-click the Outlook Express shortcut icon on the desktop. The program starts and displays its window, but this window is immediately obscured by the first dialog box of the Internet Connection Wizard. Outlook Express has detected that e-mail is not yet set up on your computer and has started the wizard to help you accomplish this task. The first dialog box looks like this:

The Outlook Express icon

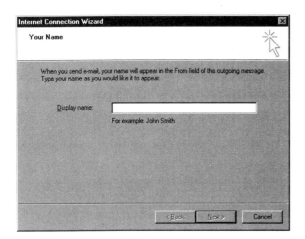

3. Enter the information the wizard requests, clicking the Next button to move from one dialog box to the next. If you have never used e-mail on your computer before, you will need to enter the information listed on the next page.

- The name you want to appear in the header of the messages you send (for example, J. Doe).

- Your full Internet e-mail address (for example, *jdoe@mail-serve.tld*).

- The Incoming Mail (POP3 or IMAP) Server name and the Outgoing Mail (SMTP) Server name supplied by your ISP (for example, *mail. mailserve.tld* for both).

- Your account name (probably the name you use when you connect to your ISP, for example, *jdoe*).

- Your password.

4. In the wizard's last dialog box, click Finish.

5. If you have previously used a different e-mail program on your computer, you may see a dialog box asking whether you want to import your existing messages and address book into Outlook Express. Complete the wizard's dialog boxes as appropriate for your situation.

6. Close Outlook Express so that the people who already had e-mail set up on their computers can rejoin us.

Starting Outlook Express

Now that everyone has set up an e-mail account, you're ready to take Outlook Express for a trial run. Follow these steps:

The Launch Outlook Express button

1. Either double-click the Outlook Express icon on the desktop or click the Launch Outlook Express button on the Quick Launch toolbar at the left end of the Windows taskbar.

About passwords

By definition, a password is a security device designed to let authorized users into an account and keep unauthorized users out. A password cannot serve this function unless it is secret. If you use a stand-alone computer to exchange personal e-mail with friends and family, the secrecy of your password may be low on your list of worries. In any other situation, you will want to ensure that your password is complicated enough that it is hard to guess it. (Combinations that include uppercase and lowercase letters and numbers are best.) But it shouldn't be so complicated that it is hard to remember without writing it down. You will want to change your password on a regular basis. (Your company or school may notify you when the change is needed.)

2. If Outlook Express displays any dialog boxes about your previous e-mail set up, respond to them accordingly. If you are not automatically connected to an e-mail server on your organization's network, you see the dialog box shown below:

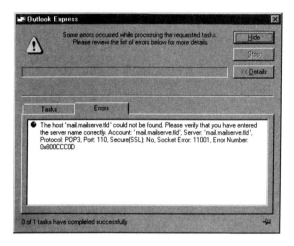

3. Click the Close button, and then choose Work Offline from the File menu.

4. Now maximize the Outlook Express window, which looks like this:

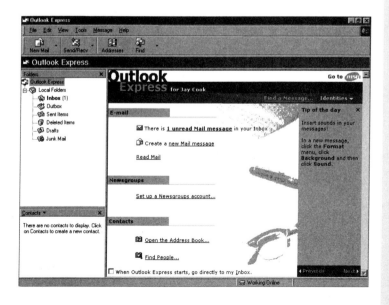

E-mail security

Your e-mail is vulnerable to snooping, as unencrypted e-mail offers about as much privacy as a postcard. It is also vulnerable to *spoofing*, as any lout can send e-mail in your name or tamper with an existing message. To prevent both problems, get a *digital ID*, composed of a *public key*, a *private key*, and a *digital signature*. Your public key is used by others to encrypt messages to you, which you decode with your private key. This two-key process is quite safe and is based on irreversible mathematical algorithms. (To encrypt a message, you need the recipient's public key, which you can get from his or her digitally signed mail.) The digital signature affirms that you are the sender and that the message has not been altered en route. Digital IDs are issued by independent agencies, who verify your identity and re-verify the issued ID at certain intervals. For more information about digital IDs and encrypted e-mail, see Internet Explorer's Help feature.

The window is divided into panes. In the top left pane, a folder list provides easy access to your mail folders. The pane on the right displays the contents of the folder selected in the folder list. The bottom left pane is reserved for a list of contacts that you will enter in the Address Book, which is where you keep information about the people you frequently send e-mail to. (See page 79 for more information about adding contacts.)

5. Click the *When Outlook Express starts, go directly to my Inbox* check box at the bottom of the right pane, and then click the *Read Mail* hyperlink in the E-mail section.

6. The contents of your Inbox folder are now displayed in two panes on the right, like this:

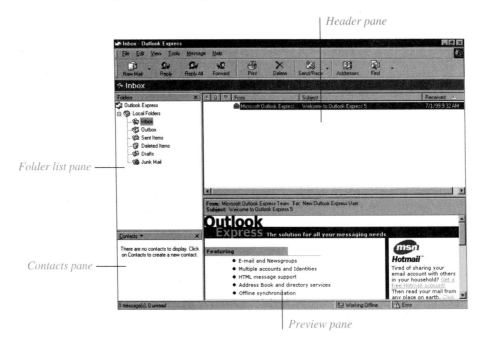

Header pane

Folder list pane

Contacts pane

Preview pane

In the top left pane, Inbox is selected in the folder list. The headers of the messages in the selected folder are displayed in the top right pane, and the message selected in that pane is previewed in the bottom right pane.

Customizing the Outlook Express Window

You can tailor the Outlook Express window in a variety of
ways to suit the way you work. Let's take a look at some of the
options:

1. Choose Layout from the View menu to display the dialog box
shown below:

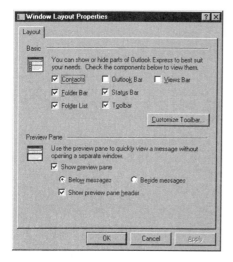

2. Click each option in turn and click Apply to see its effect. (To
see the effects of some of the options, you might have to
move the dialog box out of the way by dragging its title bar.)

3. When you're ready, select only Contacts, Folder List, Status
Bar, and Toolbar in the Basic section.

4. Click Customize Toolbar to display this dialog box:

5. Click the arrow to the right of the Text Options box, select No Text Labels, and click Close.

6. Back in the Window Layout Properties dialog box, deselect Show Preview Pane Header in the Preview Pane section. Then click OK.

Sizing panes → 7. Allocate more space to the contacts pane by pointing to the gray bar above the word *Contacts* and dragging upward to make the pane bigger.

8. Adjust the widths of the left panes by pointing to their right border and dragging to the left to make the panes narrower. Then allocate more space to the preview pane by dragging its top border upward.

Adjusting column widths → 9. Finally, adjust the widths of columns in the message header pane by dragging the borders between column headers. The results are shown here:

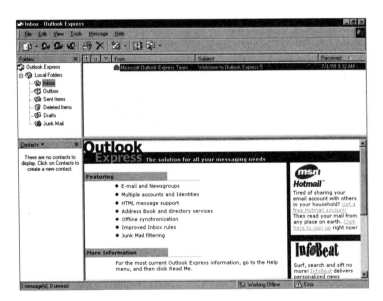

With that orientation done, it's time to move on to the next section, where we'll walk you through the necessary steps for sending e-mail messages.

Sending Messages

For this example, imagine you want to remind yourself to check on a restaurant reservation first thing in the morning. As we demonstrate, you can write messages without being connected to the Internet and then send them when you make the connection. This technique allows you to ensure that your messages say what you intended and have no embarrasing errors before you send them on their way. (Even if you don't have to worry about connect charges, it makes sense to work offline so that you are not tying up phone lines or taking up bandwidth on a network or an ISP's system. If you start a message while online and then realize it is going to take a while to finish, you can click the Work Offline button on the New Message window's toolbar.) Follow these steps to compose a message offline:

The Work Offline button

1. Click the New Message button on the toolbar to display this window:

The New Message button

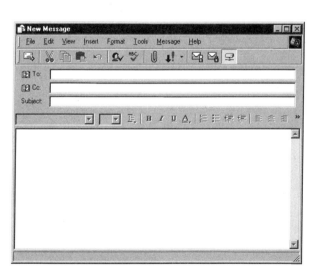

2. In the To box, type your e-mail address. (To send a message to someone else, you type his or her e-mail address. To send the same message to more than one person, you type their addresses one after the other, separated by a comma or a semicolon and a space.) Then press Tab to move to the Cc box.

Sending courtesy copies

3. To send a courtesy copy of the message, you can enter the address of the recipient in the Cc box. For this message, leave the Cc box blank by pressing Tab.

Specifying the subject

4. In the Subject box, enter *Seattle night out* and press Tab. This subject is short and to the point (see the tip below).

5. Next type the following in the message area:

   Eric said to try Pontevecchio (206-555-3989). It's a small Italian bistro just a brisk walk away from the conference site.

   Your screen now looks like this one:

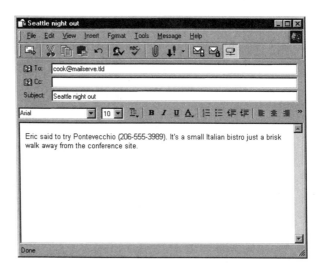

Formatting messages

If you want, you can use the buttons on the Formatting toolbar above the message area to format the message in various

Message templates

You can click the arrow to the right of the New Message button to drop down a list of templates that you can use as the basis for special messages. Selecting a template displays the New Message window with decorated "stationery" designed to complement special-occasion messages, such as party invitations or birthday greetings.

Keep the message's recipient in mind

Some people receive so many messages that they need to be able to distinguish at a glance which they should read immediately and which they can read later. A subject line like *A New Idea* tells them nothing about the content; *New slogan for Glacier Series* is much better. If the message is time-sensitive, say so by starting the Subject line with the word *Urgent*. If the message does not require any action on the part of the recipient, say so by starting the line with *FYI* (for your information). As for the message itself, avoid long paragraphs, which are hard to read on the screen. Also avoid long messages, limiting them, if possible, to one screenful of information so that the recipient can see the entire message at once.

ways. Choose Formatting Toolbar from the window's View menu to turn off the toolbar if you don't use it.

6. When you are ready to send the message, click the Send button. Because you are working offline, Outlook Express moves the message to your Outbox folder. (If you are connected to your mail server, clicking Send instantly sends the message.)

The Send button

7. If the program displays a message telling you that you can send the message later by choosing the Send And Receive command, click the Don't Show option and then click OK to close both the message box and the New Message window. Now the word *Outbox* in the folder list pane is bold and accompanied by the number 1 in parentheses to indicate that one message is waiting to be sent.

8. Click the Outbox folder to verify that the message is there, and then click the Inbox folder.

Shortcuts for Addressing Messages

After a while, you'll probably find yourself e-mailing a few people frequently. If you store their addresses in your Address Book, they will show up in the contacts pane, and you won't have to type them every time. Follow these steps to add a new contact to the address book:

1. Click the word *Contacts* at the top of the contacts pane and then click New Contact to display the dialog box shown at the top of the next page.

Adding contacts

The Address Book

You can open your Address Book at any time by clicking the Address Book button. To sort the information by first or last name, by e-mail address, or by phone number, click the appropriate column header in the Address Book window. Clicking the header again reverses the sort order (ascending vs. descending). To erase a contact or group, select the entry and click the Delete button. You can print the Address Book information by selecting the relevant entries, clicking the Print button, and choosing a print style: Memo (all data), Business Card, or Phone List. You can send an e-mail message, place a telephone call, or set up an Internet call (see page 124) to a selected contact by clicking the Actions button and making your selection from the drop-down list.

Plain text messages

By default, Outlook Express sends your messages coded with HTML (HyperText Markup Language). If you are unsure whether a contact uses an e-mail program that supports HTML, click the Send E-Mail Using Plain Text Only check box at the bottom of the Name tab in the Properties dialog box. Then all your e-mail to this contact will be sent as plain text.

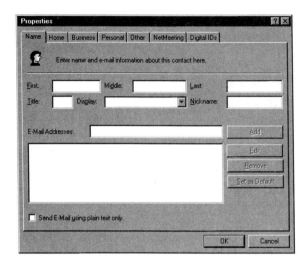

2. On the Name tab, type your first name in the First box and your last name in the Last box.

3. Adjust the entry in the Display box to reflect the way you want your name to appear in your messages.

4. In the Nickname box, type *me*.

5. In the E-Mail Addresses box, type your e-mail address and then click the Add button to move your address to the list box below. (Because you have entered only one e-mail address, Outlook Express assumes this is the one you will use by default. If you enter more than one, you can select an address and click the Set As Default button.)

6. Click OK to add yourself to the Address Book and to the list in the contacts pane. (If you don't see your name in the contacts pane, close Outlook Express and then open it again.)

Now try sending another message, this time using the contacts pane to see how it speeds up the process. Follow these steps:

Sending a message using the contacts pane

1. In the contacts pane, double-click your display name. Outlook Express opens a New Message window with your name in the To box, underlining the name to indicate that it corresponds with an entry in your Address Book.

2. Press Tab twice to move to the Subject box, type *The Henry Gallery*, and press Tab again.

3. Type *Candice says we must make time during the conference to go to the new Henry Gallery on the University campus.* Then click the Send button.

   The Outbox folder now contains two messages waiting for transmission.

Sending Contact Information in Your Messages

Outlook Express provides a simple way for you to include with your outgoing e-mail messages information about yourself that other people can easily add to their Address Books. Follow these steps to create a personal business card (also called a *vcard*, for *virtual card*) for yourself:

1. Choose Options from the Tools menu and click the Compose tab to display the dialog box shown below:

◄———————————————————

Creating a vcard

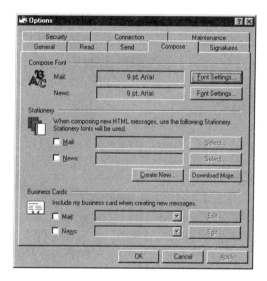

Using groups

If you frequently send messages to a set of people, you can create a group in the Address Book. Click the New button on the Address Book's toolbar and then select New Group. Assign the group a name, click Select Members, and assign people to the group. Then click OK twice. To send messages to all the group members, right-click the group's name in the contacts pane and then choose Send E-Mail.

2. In the Business Cards section at the bottom of the dialog box, click the Mail check box, click the arrow to the right of the edit box, and then select your name from the drop-down list.

3. Click Edit to open the Properties dialog box for your Address Book entry.

4. Check out some of the other tabs of the dialog box to get an idea of the kind of information you can store in the Address Book. For example, if you use e-mail primarily for business purposes, you will probably want to complete the Business tab.

5. When you are finished, click OK.

6. Back in the Options dialog box, you could click OK to attach your business card to all outgoing messages. But for our examples, deselect the Mail check box and then click OK to close the dialog box without selecting this option.

Now let's see how to use your business card:

Overriding AutoComplete

1. Click the New Message button, type *me* in the To box to send this message to yourself, and press Tab twice. (If you have a contact in your Address Book whose display name begins with *me*, AutoComplete enters that name in the To box for you. Simply press the Delete key to remove AutoComplete's portion of the name and then press Tab twice.)

The Check Names button

2. When you created a message by double-clicking your name in the contacts pane, Outlook Express underlined the address to indicate that it is in your Address Book. But the program hasn't underlined the nickname. To verify that you have typed a nickname that is associated with an e-mail address in your Address Book, click the Check Names button on the window's toolbar. Outlook Express looks up the nickname in the Address Book, substitutes the display name, and underlines it to confirm that it is associated with an Address Book entry.

3. Type *All about me!* in the Subject box, and type *Here is my business card* in the message area.

4. Choose My Business Card from the Insert menu. Outlook Express adds a business card icon to the right of the address area to pass your contact information along to the recipient of this message.

5. Click the Send button to send the message and the business card to yourself.

That's all there is to it. We tell you what to do with the business cards you receive from others on page 87.

Attaching Files to Messages

With Outlook Express, you can send files with your messages. For example, suppose you want to send the Tim Berners-Lee Web page you saved in Chapter 2 to a friend. The following steps, which use your own e-mail address instead of your friend's, demonstrate the process:

1. In the contacts pane, double-click your display name to open a New Message window. Press Tab twice to skip over the Cc box, type *Tim Berners-Lee* in the Subject box, and then press Tab again.

2. In the message area, type *As promised, here is the FAQ about the Web.* Then press Enter.

3. Click the Attach File button on the toolbar to display a dialog box in which you can select the file you want to attach to the message, as shown below:

The Attach File button

Sharing contact information with others

If you want to send information about one of your contacts to someone else, select the contact in the Address Book window and choose Export and then Business Card from the Address Book's File menu. Save the information in Business Card format in the My Documents folder. Then attach the business card file to an e-mail message just as you would any other file.

4. Move to My Documents and then to the Web Pages folder where the FAQ file is stored, and double-click the file's name. In the New Message window, *Tim Berners-Lee.htm* now appears in an Attach box that has been added below the Subject box, as shown here:

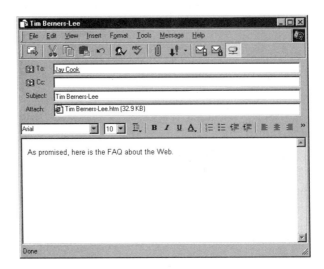

Attaching a signature

To create a signature that will appear at the bottom of your messages, choose Options from the Tools menu and click the Signatures tab. Click New and type the signature in the Edit Signature box. (Keep it short and avoid being cute.) Click Add Signatures To All Outgoing Messages and click OK. If you prefer not to add your signature to every outgoing message, leave that option turned off. When you have a message that you do want the signature added to, choose Signature from the New Message window's Insert menu.

Attaching a picture

You can easily attach a picture to a message. First choose Options from the Tools menu, and on the Send tab, check that HTML is selected in the Mail Sending Format section. Click the HTML Settings button, check that Send Pictures With Messages is selected, and click OK. In the New Message window, click an insertion point where you want the image to appear and choose Picture from the Insert menu. Click Browse and navigate to the desired image file, double-click its filename, and click OK to insert the file.

Attaching a Web page

If you want to send a hyperlink to a Web page with a message, first make sure Rich Text (HTML) is chosen on the New Message window's Format menu. In the body of the message, you can simply type a Web site's URL to create an active link to that site. Or you can select the text that will serve as the link, click the Insert Hyperlink button on the Formatting toolbar, select the resource type, enter the path to the linked site, and click OK. Then send the message in the usual way.

5. Click the Send button to store the message in the Outbox.

Sending Messages Stored in the Outbox

Unless you are permanently connected to your mail server, you now have four messages stored in the Outbox folder, waiting for you to connect to the Internet so that they can be sent on their way. Here's how to send the messages:

1. Click the Outbox folder in the folder list pane of the Outlook Express window to see the messages.

2. Click the Send And Receive All button on the toolbar. Outlook Express displays this dialog box:

The Send and Receive All button

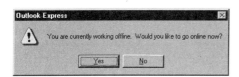

3. Click Yes. Outlook Express initiates the connection to your ISP (prompting you to enter your user name and password if necessary), sends the messages, and checks for any incoming messages.

Retrieving and Handling Messages

You can retrieve any messages that are waiting in your mailbox on your mail server by clicking the arrow to the right of the Send And Receive All button on the toolbar and selecting Receive All. (As you've seen, simply clicking the Send And Receive All button both sends any messages that are waiting in the Outbox and retrieves any incoming messages.) Usually, you will want to keep Outlook Express open while you work on the Internet so that you can receive any new messages. Outlook Express will check the server for messages according to the schedule you set on the General tab of the Options dialog box (see the adjacent tip).

When you have Outlook Express set up to retrieve messages according to a schedule, the program notifies you when you

Scheduling mail delivery

If you are connected to your ISP and running Outlook Express, by default the program checks the server every 30 minutes for new messages. You can change this schedule by choosing Options from the Outlook Express Tools menu and adjusting the Check For New Messages Every setting.

New message alert

receive a new message by displaying an envelope icon at the right end of the taskbar. (It may also play a sound to alert you to the new arrival.) Here's how to manually retrieve messages:

1. Click the Inbox folder in the folder list pane to display the new message headers in the top right pane. (If you don't see the new messages in your Inbox, click the Send And Receive All button again.) Your screen looks like this:

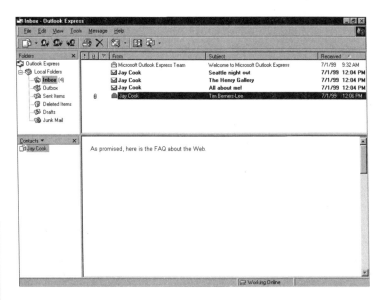

Now take a closer look at the message header pane. Each message includes the sender's name, the subject, and the date and time you received the message. When you have not yet displayed a message, an unopened envelope is shown next to the sender's name, and the message header is displayed in bold. An exclamation mark in the first column indicates that the message is urgent (see page 89). A paper clip in the second column indicates that the message has an attachment, and a flag in the third column indicates that you have flagged the message to remind you to do something with it (see the adjacent tip).

Here's how to read a message:

1. Click the Seattle Night Out message. Outlook Express displays the message in the preview pane below. After a few seconds,

Marking messages

By default, if you display a message in the preview pane for 5 seconds, Outlook Express presumes you have read it, opens the message's envelope icon, and changes its font style. (To change this setting, choose Options from the Tools menu, click the Read tab, and adjust the Mark Message Read setting.) You can manually mark a message as read or unread by right-clicking its header and then choosing Mark As Read or Mark As Unread from the shortcut menu. You can also draw attention to a message by putting a flag icon to the left of its header. Simply select the header and choose Flag Message from the Message menu. Choosing the command again toggles it off.

the unopened envelope changes to an opened one, and the font's style changes from bold to regular.

2. Double-click the All About Me message to open it in a window like this one:

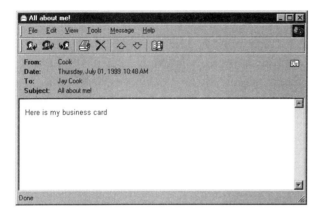

3. Next click the card icon to the right of the From line and choose Open to display this dialog box:

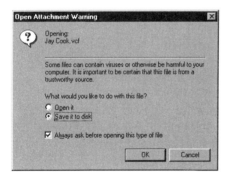

4. Because you know the source of this file, click Open It and then click OK. Outlook Express displays the business card's information in a Properties dialog box with an Add To Address Book button. If you click this button, the information in the dialog box becomes editable, so that you can add or change the information before clicking OK to create an entry for this contact in your Address Book and in your contacts pane.

Mailing lists

Once you become proficient with e-mail, you might want to explore *mailing lists*, or *listservs* (for list servers). Mailing lists enable people with similar interests to relay information about a specific topic. To find out what mailing lists are available, connect to your ISP, start Internet Explorer, and then move to the Yahoo Web site. Click *Computers And Internet*, then *Internet*, and then *Mailing Lists*. Now you can scroll through the subjects and check out any that interest you. If you want to subscribe to any of them, send a *subscription address* to the Listserve program that administers the mailing list; the directions for doing so should be spelled out in the mailing list's description. Once you've subscribed to a mailing list, you receive its messages along with your regular e-mail in your Inbox. You can contribute by sending messages in the usual way. While it is tempting to subscribe to multiple mailing lists, you should select them carefully; subscribing to a few active mailing lists can swamp your Inbox.

5. This information is already in your Address Book, so click Cancel. Then close the message window.

6. Now double-click the Tim Berners-Lee message to open it in a window.

Opening an attached file

7. Double-click the name of the file in the Attach line. Again Outlook Express displays the Open Attachment Warning dialog box.

8. This time, leave the Save It To Disk option selected and click OK. Outlook Express displays a Save Attachment As dialog box that is similar to the Save As dialog box.

9. Save the file in the My Documents folder and then close the message window.

Replying to Messages

Suppose this message is from a colleague and requires a response. Follow these steps to send a reply:

The Reply To Sender button

1. With the Tim Berners-Lee message selected, click the Reply To Sender button on the toolbar to open a window like the one shown here:

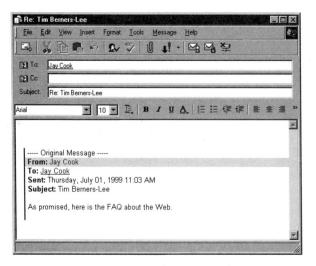

The Reply To All button

Notice that the To and Subject boxes are already filled in. (Clicking the Reply To All button displays a similar window, except that the To box contains not only the address of the original sender but also those of all recipients of carbon copies.) Notice also that the original message appears at the bottom of the message area preceded by a vertical line. Outlook Express has inserted this text because the Include Message In Reply option is selected by default on the Send tab of the dialog box displayed when you choose Options from the Outlook Express Tools menu.

2. Type *Thanks. Great stuff!* and click the Send button. Outlook Express sends the reply if you are connected to the Internet; if you are working offline, it puts it in the Outbox.

3. So that you can see how the reply looks, click the Send And Receive All button and check the new message when it arrives.

Forwarding Messages

If you receive a message that you think will be of interest to a colleague, you can forward the message with a few mouse clicks. Here's how:

1. Click the *Seattle night out* message and then click the Forward button on the toolbar to display this window:

The Forward button

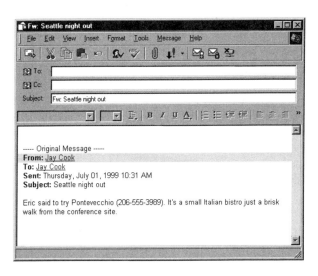

2. For demonstration purposes, type *me* in the To box.

3. Click the arrow to the right of the Set Priority button and select High Priority from the drop-down list.

The Set Priority button

4. Click an insertion point in the message area, type *Here's where we'll have dinner on Friday night!*, press Enter, and click the Send button on the toolbar.

Deleting Messages

In the early days of e-mail, people would often hang on to old e-mail messages so that they had a record of their senders' addresses. Because it is easy to add e-mail addresses to your Address Book, that particular reason for keeping old messages no longer exists. (In fact, Outlook Express automatically creates an Address Book entry using the e-mail address from any message to which you respond.) After you have finished reading many of your messages, you will probably want to delete them. To demonstrate how to delete messages, we'll show you how to clean up the Sent Items folder, but the procedure is the same for any folder. Follow these steps:

Automatic Address Book entries

1. Click the Sent Items folder in the folder list pane to display the headers of all the messages you have sent. (Outlook Express stores copies of your sent messages in this folder because the Save Copy Of Sent Messages option is selected by default on the Send tab of the Options dialog box.)

2. Select the first message, hold down the Shift key, and click the last message to select everything in the folder. Then click the Delete button on the toolbar.

The Delete button

3. Click the Deleted Items folder in the folder list pane. The Sent Items messages have been transferred there, allowing you to change your mind about deleting them.

4. Right-click the Deleted Items folder, choose Empty 'Deleted Items' Folder from the shortcut menu, and click Yes to confirm that you want to discard them.

Organizing Messages

When you first started Outlook Express, the program provided six folders: Inbox, Outbox, Sent Items, Deleted Items, Drafts, and Junk Mail. In addition to these program-generated folders, you can create folders of your own to help organize messages in logical ways. (Some people prefer to create folders in which to store all their messages so that the Inbox acts as a

Moving among unread messages

When you have several messages in your Inbox, it is easy to catch up with the unread mail. Simply choose Next and then Next Unread Message from the View menu. You can also press Ctrl+U to jump from one unread message to another.

temporary receptacle for new messages only.) Let's create a folder and move some messages into it now:

1. Right-click Inbox in the folder list pane and choose New Folder from the shortcut menu to display this dialog box:

Creating folders

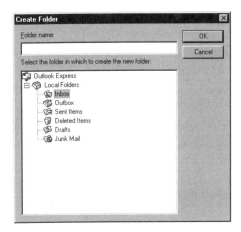

2. Type *Seattle Conference* in the Folder Name edit box and press Enter.

3. In the Inbox, select the *Seattle night out* message and drag it to the Seattle Conference folder.

Moving messages

4. Here's another way to move messages. Right-click the *FW: Seattle night out* message, choose Move To Folder from the shortcut menu, select the Seattle Conference folder in the Move dialog box, and click OK.

5. Click the Seattle Conference folder in the folder list pane to display the messages in their new location, like this (we've widened the folder list pane):

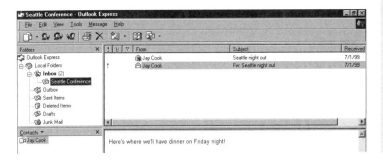

The Drafts folder

When you are composing an important e-mail message (or one that's very long), you may need to pause to do a little research or maybe just to take a break. You can choose the File menu's Save command to store the unfinished message in the Drafts folder. Then when you're ready to resume, double-click the message in that folder to reopen the message window with all the information you have already entered intact. You can then finish the message and send it on its way.

Finding People's E-Mail Addresses

Once you have e-mail, you'll probably use it whenever you can for both business and personal communications. The one big stumbling block will be obtaining the necessary e-mail addresses. Suppose you've been asked to research the feasibility of exporting your company's products to East Asia, and you remember hearing that a former colleague recently toured several East Asian countries with a trade delegation. You want to touch base with her to see if she can point you to some information sources. Or suppose you have been thinking lately how different your life would have been if one of your teachers hadn't coaxed you into taking higher-level math courses rather than sticking with easy courses. You want to let him know how you're doing and to thank him for taking an interest when he did. How can you send e-mail messages to these people if you don't know their e-mail addresses?

One way to track down the e-mail addresses of individuals and companies is through Internet "white pages" directories. Access to several of these directories is built into Outlook Express, and in this section, you'll use one called *Bigfoot*. Follow these steps:

The Find button

1. Click the arrow to the right of the Find button and select People from the drop-down list to display this dialog box:

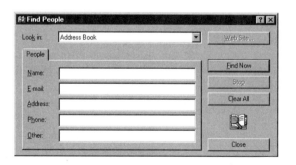

Other ways to find addresses

When Outlook Express is selected in the folder list pane (see page 74), you can click the *Find People* hyperlink in the pane on the right to display the Find People dialog box. You can also click the Address Book button on the toolbar and then click the Find People button. In Windows, you can choose Find and then People from the Start menu.

2. Click the arrow at the right end of the Look In box and select Bigfoot Internet Directory Service from the drop-down list. (For more information about the selected directory, you can click the Web Site button in the Find People dialog box to display the directory's home page.)

3. Type a name in the Name box and click Find Now. For example, here is the result when you enter *Scott Adams* (the creator of the Dilbert cartoon strip):

This type of search is not infallible—there's a chance you'll pick a name that is not in a directory or that yields no listings that seem to be the person you are looking for. Another drawback: the results list can be pretty long, and there is often no way to figure out which, if any, of the addresses is the right one.

4. In this case, select scottadams@aol.com, click Add To Address Book to open a Properties dialog box, and then click OK to add Scott Adams to your Address Book.

5. Click Close to close the Find People dialog box.

6. Close Outlook Express and disconnect from your ISP.

Style and Etiquette

We thought it would be appropriate to end this discussion by passing along a few e-mail conventions. (Your company may have its own set of *do's* and *don'ts*, especially for communications with customers.)

People are often much more casual about the tone and language they use in e-mail messages than in letters. By and large, a less

Other directories

If Bigfoot doesn't yield the results you want, try Yahoo, Infospace, Switchboard, Verisign, or WhoWhere. To select the particular directory you want to search, simply click the arrow to the right of the Look In box and then click the name of the directory.

formal approach is appropriate, unless you are communicating with customers or the company CEO. However, *less formal* doesn't mean *sloppy*; you should still check your spelling and grammar. And *less formal* doesn't mean *unthinking*; you should still be careful about how you express yourself. Many people think of e-mail as an electronic form of conversation. But without facial expressions, body language, and voice inflections, words in an e-mail message can easily be misunderstood. To mitigate this problem, and to cope with the fact that many people still send and receive messages in plain text (no bold, italic, or underlining), the online community has adopted the following techniques for adding emphasis and indicating humor, amazement, or anger:

- **Capital letters.** Generally, capital letters should be used sparingly in messages because they add varying degrees of emphasis. Using initial capital letters draws attention to words Without Stressing Them. Writing an entire word in capital letters DOES stress the word. An entire phrase or sentence in capital letters is very emphatic and SHOULD BE AVOIDED unless appropriate for the context of the message.

WRITING AN ENTIRE PARAGRAPH OR MESSAGE IN CAPITAL LETTERS MAKES IT HARD TO READ AND IS THE E-MAIL EQUIVALENT OF SHOUTING. IT MAY BE INTERPRETED AS RUDE. EVEN IF YOU HAVE A LEGITIMATE GRIPE, THINK TWICE BEFORE FIRING OFF A MESSAGE IN ALL CAPS.

Sending rude messages, called *flaming*, is generally frowned on and can provoke irrational responses.

- **Punctuation.** The asterisk can be used to add *mild* emphasis to a specific word. The exclamation mark in conjunction with capital letters can ensure that a !!!VERY IMPORTANT POINT!!! gets made. Strings of question marks and exclamation marks denote confusion, but strings of other punctuation marks are commonly interpreted as placeholders for swear words, as in *??!!??Why did you call him a $%&@*??!!??*

These guidelines apply not only to e-mail but to other forms of online communication, such as newsgroups, which we discuss in Chapter 4.

Emoticons

Also called *smileys*, emoticons are combinations of characters which, when viewed sideways, resemble facial expressions. They were all the rage at one time but have now fallen out of fashion (thank goodness!). In case you come across them in the messages you receive, here's a list of some of the more common emoticons and their meanings:

:-)	I'm happy
:-(	I'm not happy
:-c	I'm very unhappy
;-)	I'm kidding (wink)
:-D	I'm laughing
:-o	I'm amazed
<:-<	I'm angry
:-@	I'm screaming
%-)	I'm confused

BUILDING PROFICIENCY

After completing the chapters in Part Two, you will know enough to put Internet Explorer to work, streamlining your Web access and facilitating communication both within your company and with the outside world. In Chapter 4, you take a look at newsgroups, a valuable source of information about a wide variety of topics. In Chapter 5, you focus on NetMeeting as a versatile means of Internet communication. Finally, in Chapter 6, you customize Internet Explorer to make it more convenient and to increase your efficiency.

Participating in Newsgroups

We use Outlook Express to show you how to find newsgroups that match your interests, how to subscribe to those you want to visit regularly, and how to select and read articles. Then we demonstrate how to follow up on articles and how to post new ones.

The skills you learn for selecting and participating in a newsgroup can be applied to any group on any topic, from medical conditions to philosophy and from musical groups to computer operating systems.

Tasks performed and concepts covered:

Post articles and follow-ups using the New Message and Reply To Sender buttons

View related articles as threads

Subscribe to the newsgroups you want to participate in

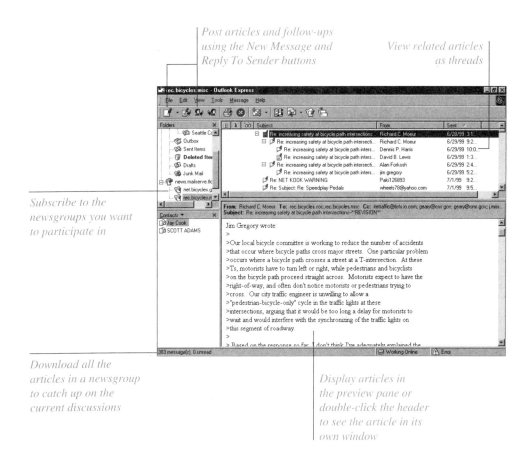

Download all the articles in a newsgroup to catch up on the current discussions

Display articles in the preview pane or double-click the header to see the article in its own window

What are newsgroups? →

Newsgroups is a term used to refer to a vast collection of public discussion groups, organized around literally thousands of topics, that are accessible via the Internet. (They are also accessible in other ways, but we won't go into that here.) Newsgroups are the closest thing the Internet has to a community bulletin board, where you can check out the latest messages about a mind-boggling number of subjects. You can passively read these messages or actively participate in a discussion by contributing your own messages in a way that is very similar to sending e-mail. As an active participant, you can ask questions, help resolve other people's problems, gossip, rave about a hero, debate a Supreme Court decision, exchange recipes, get automobile recommendations, research any subject that is dear to your wallet or your heart, and generally while away many an hour interacting with others who share your interests or needs.

News reader programs →

In this chapter, you will learn how to use the *news reader* component of Outlook Express to join a couple of the online conversations that are available through Usenet, the largest of the newsgroup systems. You will learn how to determine which newsgroups are likely to focus on topics that interest you and which ones are most likely to cater to "fringe" tastes. You will also investigate how to join a newsgroup gracefully and how to become a valued member of the groups where you decide to concentrate your time.

Newsgroup Concepts

Internet service providers can use one of their servers to carry all or some of the Usenet newsgroups, and many ISPs also carry other newsgroups, including regional ones that cater to local interests. However, some ISPs don't carry newsgroups at all. As long as your ISP has a news server, you can tap into this huge reservoir of information and social interaction without any additional software, because Outlook Express includes the *Network News Transfer Protocol* (or *NNTP*) needed to participate in newsgroups.

Newsgroups vs. mailing lists

The difference between these two Internet resources lies in their delivery methods. With a mailing list, copies of the messages on the list are made for each subscriber and are sent to his or her mailbox. (See page 87 for information about mailing lists.) With a newsgroup, the group's articles are stored on the news server, and you make your own copies of the articles only if you want to keep them.

So how do newsgroups operate? Suppose you work for a mail-order company that sells equipment and accessories for bicyclists. Part of your job is to research trends that affect the company's target market, so you want to participate in newsgroups frequented by the bicycling enthusiasts who might be interested in your products. You connect to your ISP, start Outlook Express, and select an appropriate newsgroup, where you can read any relevant messages, called *articles*, that other people have already contributed. Then when you are ready to become an active participant, you can *post* new articles and *follow up* on articles posted by others.

← How newsgroups work

← Articles

← Posting and following up

Newsgroups are usually organized hierarchically by topic (see the next section for more information). Most newsgroups are *unmoderated*, meaning that they allow anyone to post or follow up on articles. Some are *moderated*, meaning that they require that all submissions—both new articles and follow-ups—be sent to the group's moderator for approval. The moderator then posts those that he or she feels are relevant and useful. Articles within newsgroups are organized into clusters, called *threads*, that consist of the original article and any follow-ups. So instead of reading newsgroups chronologically, you read subject-based threads that may have evolved over several days or even weeks as various people added their comments.

← Unmoderated vs. moderated newsgroups

← Threads

Newsgroup Hierarchies

The more traditional newsgroups are organized into categories, which are divided into subcategories, which are in turn divided into sub-subcategories, and so on. Their names follow this hierarchy, identifying first the category, then the subcategory, and then the sub-subcategory, with each level separated from the next by a period. Sound confusing? Here's a typical Usenet newsgroup name:

misc.education.home-school

Reading from left to right, the general category is *misc* (for *miscellaneous*), the subcategory is *education*, and the sub-subcategory is *home-school*.

About Usenet

Like the Internet, Usenet is not a *thing*, but it's not a *network*, either. It's a loose association of news administrators who allow their servers to function as Usenet distribution sites, called *newsfeeds*.

Because ISPs can decide which newsgroups to carry on their servers, not all providers carry all available groups. So that we can be reasonably sure you will have access to the newsgroups used in our examples, we focus on Usenet newsgroups, which are divided into general categories like these:

Primary Usenet categories →

biz	Business (commercial)
comp	Computer-related
K12	Teaching and students
misc	Miscellaneous topics
news	Usenet information
rec	Recreation and leisure activities
sci	Science (except for computer science, which is in *comp*)
soc	Social issues and all kinds of socializing
talk	Topic-based, often heated discussions

You might also have access to the catch-all *alt* (for *alternative*) category of Usenet newsgroups, which includes everything that doesn't fit into the other categories, such as lifestyles, hobbies, religions, support groups, and fan clubs. You'll explore newsgroup hierarchies as you work with the Outlook Express news reader, but first, you have one procedural step to take care of.

Setting Up Outlook Express for News

Blocking newsgroups
If you want to be able to browse through newsgroups without being confronted by smutty articles, you can use a filtering program to block the display of any newsgroup containing this type of material. As we discuss on page 167, programs such as Cyber Patrol and SurfWatch come with regularly updated databases of offending Web sites, newsgroups, and FTP servers. They work by simply hiding anything in the database from view. You can also use Outlook Express's built-in filtering capabilities; see the tip on page 108.

If you work for a large organization or you access the Internet through a school server, your computer may already be set up to access newsgroups. If that is the case, you can skip this section and jump to page 102, where you learn how to browse through the newsgroups that are available to you. If newsgroup access is not yet set up on your computer, you need to tell Outlook Express the host address of the server that handles newsgroups and some information about yourself. Assuming that you have already completed the steps for setting up Outlook Express for e-mail (see page 71), follow these steps:

1. Obtain the address of your news server from your ISP.

2. Connect to your ISP and start Outlook Express.

3. Click Outlook Express in the left pane to display these options in the right pane:

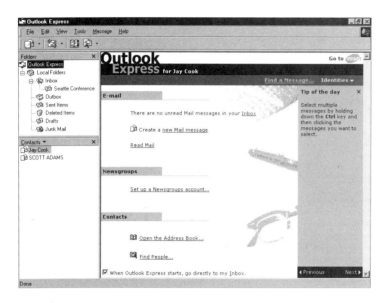

4. Click Set Up A Newsgroups Account in the right pane to start the Internet Connection Wizard, which displays this dialog box:

Setting news options

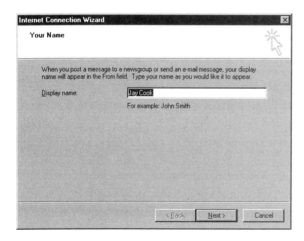

5. Enter the following information, clicking the Next button to move from one dialog box to the next:

• Your first and last name (for example, *Jill Doe*), or the name that you want others to see when you post or follow up on articles.

- Your full Internet e-mail address (for example, *jdoe@mail-serve.tld*).

- The name of your news (NNTP) server (for example, *news.-mailserve.tld*). If your ISP requires you to log onto the news server, click the check box at the bottom of this dialog box.

6. In the wizard's last dialog box, click Finish to save your news settings. You then see this dialog box:

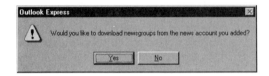

7. Click No to close the dialog box, then close Outlook Express and, if necessary, disconnect from your ISP.

Exploring Usenet Newsgroups

For efficiency, every Usenet user should read a few specific newsgroups before setting off on any broader exploration. The *news* newsgroups category offers you a wealth of information about how to get started with newsgroups, as well as some interesting historical Usenet background. You'll benefit from reading the articles in the *news.announce.newusers* group before you post any articles of your own, and you might want to read those in the *news.answers* group to get information about a specific group you are interested in. Later in this chapter you will learn how to save these articles on your hard disk as files so that you can read them offline. These articles were written by newsgroup veterans and offer sound advice on how to participate in newsgroups. (They reinforce the information we provide in this chapter.)

Read these

You probably don't need to bother reading the articles in the *news.newusers.questions* newsgroup. Often these articles are posted by people who haven't taken the time to read *news.-announce.newusers* and *news.answers* articles, and who can't wait to post something—*anything*—to a newsgroup. At any point in time, this group might contain a few thousand articles, most of which either ask questions already answered by articles in the other two *news* newsgroups (a big no-no) or ask questions that should be posted in a different newsgroup (an even bigger no-no). Other articles are presumably someone's idea of a joke or someone's attempt at being risqué or downright shocking. At best they are immature, and at worst they are offensive. The only use you will probably find for the articles in this newsgroup is that they provide examples of what *not* to do in other newsgroups if you want to avoid the scorn of the newsgroup community.

Now that you have an idea of what to expect, let's start exploring. Follow these steps:

1. Connect to your ISP and start Outlook Express.

2. Choose Newsgroups from the Tools menu. You then see a Downloading Newsgroups message box. Downloading the entire list of groups can take some time, depending on the number of available groups and your connection speed. Once the list of groups is downloaded and saved in a file on your hard drive, you see this Newsgroup Subscriptions dialog box:

Downloading the newsgroup list

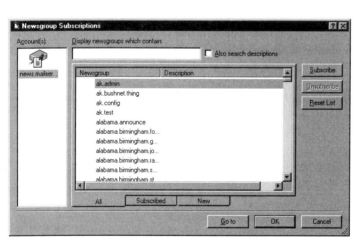

You select the newsgroups you want to read and subscribe to in the newsgroup pane. Double-clicking a newsgroup downloads the newsgroup's articles, and the right pane of the Outlook Express window then divides into two panes that resemble those of the Inbox, with the article headers at the top and a

Searching newsgroups with DejaNews

When you want to search for a particular topic, your best bet is to use DejaNews, which you will find at *www.dejanews.com*. As an example, when we entered the keywords *"bike carriers"*, Deja-News produced 11 articles from several different newsgroups, including *rec.bicycles.tech* and *alt.autos.nissan*.

preview of the selected article at the bottom. In the next section, you will see what newsgroups are available and learn how to move around.

Browsing Newsgroups

Because the *news* newsgroups are a good place for newcomers to get their feet wet, let's take a look now at some of the articles in the *news.announce.newusers* group. (If this group is not available, use *news.answers* instead.) Try this:

Narrowing down the list

1. Type *news* in the Display Newsgroups Which Contain edit box. Now the list box shows only the newsgroups that contain the word *news* in their names.

Displaying newsgroup contents

2. Scroll the list box until you see *news.announce.newusers*. (You may have to widen the Newsgroup column to see the entire name. Simply double-click the border between the Newsgroup and Description headers.) Select the newsgroup and click the Go To button. Outlook Express retrieves the list of the group's articles from your news server and displays their headers in the top right pane of the Outlook Express window.

3. Display more of the article headers by dragging the borders of the panes and column headers so that the window looks something like this:

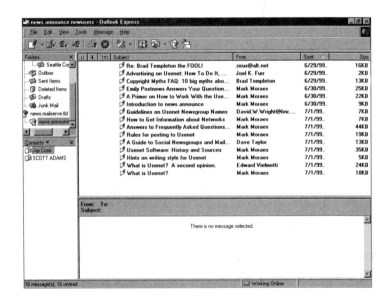

In the top right pane are columns for the subject, the sender's name, the date and time the article was posted and the size of the article. To the left of the Subject column are three columns for indicating which articles have attachments, which you want to download for offline reading, and which you want to watch for further developments. When you have not yet read an article, the header is displayed in bold type.

4. In the top pane, click an article header, such as *Introduction to news.announce*. Outlook Express displays the article in the preview pane with a header bar, much like an e-mail message header, across the top. (By the way, the list of articles on your screen will be different from ours because the articles in newsgroups change constantly. ISPs set expiration policies that range from one day to a few weeks for each newsgroup, and articles are automatically removed according to those expiration policies. Because the *news.announce.newusers* news group is an important reservoir of Usenet information, its articles are regularly reposted to the newsgroup. Even so, your list won't be exactly the same as ours. The articles you'll see in other newsgroups will also vary from those on our screens.)

Displaying articles

Expiring articles

5. Enlarge the preview pane by dragging its top border up, and scroll the article to see its information. The header and preview panes now look something like this:

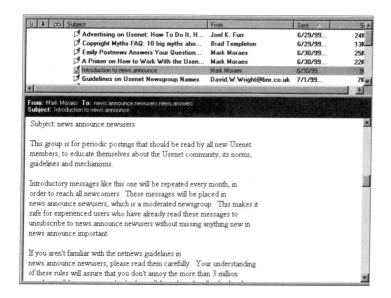

Saving Articles to Read Offline

The *Introduction* article is pretty long, and you don't want to spend time reading it online. You could choose Print from the File menu to print the article, but you don't really need a paper copy. Instead, let's save the article as a file so that you can read it later. (If you clicked a different article, save it instead.)

1. With the article displayed in the preview pane of the Outlook Express window, choose Save As from the File menu.

2. Next type *news.announce* as the filename, and change the Save As Type setting to Text Files. Create a folder called *News Articles* in your My Documents folder, open that folder, and click Save to save the file.

Now you can read the article at your leisure by opening it in any word processing program. You should glance through all the headers in *news.announce.newusers* and then save and read the articles you're interested in. Then do the same for any articles that interest you in the *news.answers* group.

Exploring Other Available Newsgroups

Having practiced with the *news* newsgroups, you can now take a look at some other newsgroups:

The Newsgroups button

1. Click the Newsgroups button on the toolbar to open the Newsgroup Subscriptions dialog box shown earlier on page 103.

2. Scroll the groups list to see the abundance of newsgroups. Then scroll to *news.lists.misc*, select it, and click Go To.

3. When Outlook Express asks whether you want to subscribe to *news.announce.newusers* before moving to *news.lists.misc*, click the Don't Ask Me This Again check box and then click No. Outlook Express then retrieves the *news.lists.misc* articles from your news server. (If the group has no posted articles, click the Newsgroup button and select *news.answers* instead.)

4. Each article preceded by a plus sign has hidden follow-up articles about the same topic, and the entire topic is a thread. If you can, click the plus sign to the left of *List Of Periodic Informational Postings* to display all the articles in that thread.

About the *.answers newsgroups

When you first check out the contents of a newsgroup, we recommend that you look for an *answers* subcategory to find out what the newsgroup traditionally covers and what the rules for participation are. (All the *.answers* articles should also be posted in *news.answers*.)

Otherwise, click the plus sign of any thread that interests you. Notice that the lower-level articles are indented under the top-level article.

5. Adjust the panes' sizes and then click the header of one of the follow ups to display it in the preview pane. For example, we went in search of a newsgroup about bicycling.

6. Scroll the article to see its contents, which resemble these:

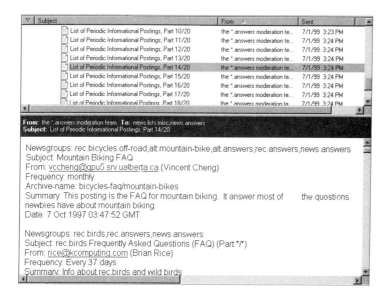

All the *Informational Postings* articles follow this format. They list, alphabetically, the Usenet newsgroups that provide FAQs or other information about themselves. With so many newsgroups to choose from, it's hard to find those that cover topics you're interested in. The *Informational Postings* articles are one place to start looking. These and other articles found in the *news* newsgroup can shed some light on the structure of the Usenet newsgroups so that you can start looking for what you need in the primary Usenet categories (see the list on page 100). It's up to you to check out any other newsgroups available through your ISP.

Subscribing to Newsgroups

When you find a newsgroup you want to participate in, or at least check regularly for new articles, you can *subscribe* to

Newsgroup acronyms

Here are some of the acronyms used most frequently by newsgroup participants:

BTW	By the way
IMHO	In my humble opinion
OTOH	On the other hand
ROTFL	Rolling on the floor, laughing
RTFM	Read the *fill-in-the-blank* manual
WRT	With respect to
YMMV	Your mileage (experience) may vary

that newsgroup. Don't worry: subscribing doesn't mean you have to fork over any money. You subscribe to a newsgroup to tell Outlook Express that you have more than a passing interest in it. You can then display only the newsgroups to which you have subscribed.

As a demonstration of how to subscribe to a newsgroup, we will use a bicycling newsgroup. First you need to find a newsgroup frequented by bicyclists:

Finding newsgroups

1. Although some people make their living as professional bike racers, for the majority of people, bicycling is a hobby. Start by clicking the Newsgroups button to open the Newsgroup Subscriptions dialog box, and then scrolling the list of newsgroups until you see *rec.bicycles* (for *recreation.bicycles*).

2. The *rec.bicycles* newsgroup has a few sub-subcategories, but you're interested in general bicycling topics. Click the *rec.bicycles.misc* newsgroup to select it and click the Subscribe button on the right to subscribe. Outlook Express flags the group with an icon.

Now subscribe to a couple of other sources of related bicycling information and display only the subscribed groups. Try this:

1. Type *bicycles* in the Display Newsgroups Which Contain edit box to check the rest of the newsgroup list for groups of interest. The list looks like this:

Filtering articles

Once you get to know a newsgroup and its regular participants, you can apply filters that will ensure that articles matching criteria you specify are treated in specific ways. Select the newsgroup you want to filter, choose Message Rules and then News from the Tools menu, specify the criteria for filtering, and apply the rule. For example, you can specify that all new articles in the *rec.bicycles.misc* group that contain the word *seat* in the Subject line are displayed in purple.

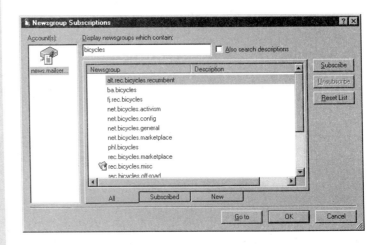

2. Subscribe to two more groups.

3. Now click the Subscribed tab, which appears as shown below. (If your subscribed newsgroups didn't all include the word *bicycles*, you would need to delete the entry in the Display Newsgroups Which Contain edit box and then press Enter to display all the groups.)

For demonstration purposes, we might as well show you how to unsubscribe from a newsgroup. Try this:

1. Make sure you are on the Subscribed tab of the Newsgroup Subscriptions dialog box.

2. Select one of the two newsgroups you just subscribed to and click the Unsubscribe button. Outlook Express removes the icon from that group.

Controlling the Display of Articles

Let's check out a few of the articles in the *rec.bicycles.misc* newsgroup:

1. Click *rec.bicycles.misc* in the Newsgroup column and click Go To to display its articles in the header pane.

2. Widen the folder list pane and notice that the number of articles currently posted to this group is displayed in the parentheses next to the newsgroup name. The number of articles downloaded, the number you have not yet read, and the

Checking the numbers

You can click your news account entry in the folder list pane to see a list of subscribed newsgroups in the right pane with the total number of articles that have been downloaded and the number you have not read for each one. If you keep up with the articles in a subscribed newsgroup, you can tell whether anything new has been posted since your last visit just by looking at this list. Then you can judge whether to display a newsgroup's articles.

number remaining to be downloaded are listed at the right end of the status bar.

3. Widen the top right pane and scroll through the list, clicking the headers of any articles of interest to display the article in the preview pane. As you have already seen, Outlook Express indicates that the article has been read by changing its type.

4. If you prefer to read an article in a separate window rather than in the preview window, double-click its header to display its text in a window like this one:

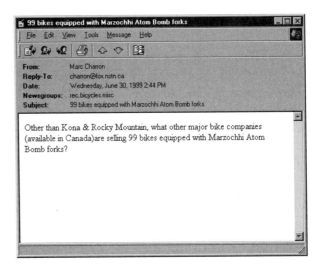

Getting a handle on large newsgroups

When you first start reading a newsgroup, the number of articles can seem overwhelming. To start with, you might want to mark all the articles as read by choosing the Mark All Read command from the Edit menu. Then you can read all new articles posted from today on, without feeling compelled to go back and read existing articles. (Usenet wisdom has it that anything worth discussing will come up again, and you can catch it next time around.)

By default, Outlook Express downloads and displays the headers of the 300 newest articles. Suppose you have read these messages and you now want to see others that you haven't read. Here's what you do:

1. Click the headers of a dozen or so articles that don't have plus signs beside them, pausing long enough on each one for it to change from bold to regular type.

2. Choose Current View and then Hide Read Messages from the View menu.

3. Now scroll the list of articles, noticing that all those you clicked in step 1 have now disappeared from the list.

4. Repeat step 1 for the next several *rec.bicycles.misc* articles.

5. Now click your other subscribed newsgroup in the folder list pane and then click *rec.bicycles.misc* again. The headers for the articles you clicked in step 4 have disappeared from the header pane.

6. To retrieve more headers, choose Get Next 300 Headers from the Tools menu. As Outlook Express downloads the headers, it displays in the status bar the number of articles available and the number you have not yet read.

◄ Downloading more articles

As you scrolled through the list of *rec.bicycles.misc* articles, you probably noticed all the threads indicated by plus signs. Let's read a thread:

1. Click the plus sign preceding a thread that does not begin with *Re:*, such as the one shown here:

◄ Reading threads

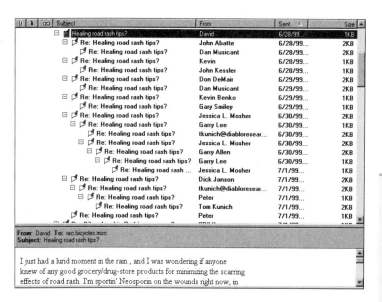

The *Re:* in the headers of the indented articles indicate that they are responses to the top-level article.

2. Click the plus sign preceding the header of a thread that does begin with *Re:*. For example, we clicked the plus sign preceding the *Re: increasing safety at bicycle path intersections* thread and then selected the top-level article shown on the next page.

Downloading more headers

Outlook Express can retrieve a maximum of 1000 headers at a time. When you display a newsgroup, by default the program retrieves 300 headers. To increase this number, choose Options from the Tools menu and on the Read tab, change the setting in the Get box. The Get Next 300 Headers command on the Tools menu then changes to reflect the new setting. To download the articles themselves, not just the headers, choose Synchronize All from the Tools menu.

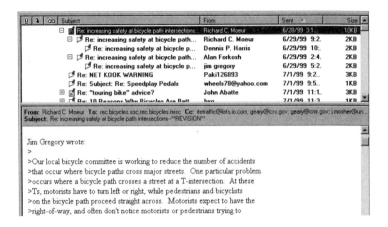

The *Re:* in the top-level header indicates that this article and those that are indented under it are responses to an earlier article that is no longer part of the thread because it has expired (see page 105).

3. Click one of the lower-level articles in the thread to display it in the preview pane.

Marking a thread as read

4. You've read enough of this thread to know that it is of no interest to you, so choose Mark Conversation As Read from the Edit menu. The entire thread is marked as read, even though you displayed only a couple of its articles.

Suppose you have read all the articles and you want to follow up on some of them, so you don't want "read" articles to be removed if you switch to another group. Follow these steps:

Displaying all articles

1. Choose Current View and then Show All Messages from the View menu and press Ctrl+Home to move to the first header in the top right pane. The articles you have read reappear.

Marking all articles as read

2. Choose Mark All Read from the Edit menu to mark the entire newsgroup as read.

OK, so now all the headers are displayed and they are all marked as read. But how do you identify those you want to follow up on? You can mark them as unread so that only they appear in the list in bold type, and you can then jump from unread article to unread article. Try this:

1. Choose Sort By and then Sort Descending from the View menu to show the most recent articles first in the header pane.

Sorting articles

2. Press Ctrl+Home. Then click the header of an article in order to display its text in the preview pane.

3. Choose Mark As Unread from the Edit menu.

Marking articles as unread

4. Repeat steps 2 and 3 to mark a few more articles as unread.

5. Now press Ctrl+Home, select the message at the top of the list, and choose Next and then Next Unread Message from the View menu to jump to the first "unread" article.

6. Press Ctrl+U to jump to the second unread article.

7. With the second article displayed in the preview pane and without quitting Outlook Express, disconnect from your ISP. (You shouldn't be connected for the rest of this chapter.)

Having read a few articles contributed by others, let's see how you might contribute some of your own.

Posting Articles

The procedure for posting articles to a newsgroup is relatively simple. The etiquette involved can be another matter, depending on the nature of the newsgroup you want to post in. Some newsgroups are inflammatory and nothing you can say will turn up the heat any higher. Others are informal and forgiving of the mistakes *newbies* (new users) can make. But the most informative and useful newsgroups are often those that have been around for a while and whose participants get irritated when newcomers barge in without bothering to learn their rules. These rules are perfectly reasonable and are designed to avoid wasting everyone's time, so bear them in mind:

- Read the newsgroup's FAQ if it has one (for Usenet newsgroups, look in *news.answers* or in the category's *.answers* newsgroup). You may have noticed that the FAQs described

Watching and ignoring

You can select the header of an article you are particularly interested in and choose Watch Conversation from the Message menu to put a glasses icon in the Watch/Ignore column of the header pane and change the color of the header. Choose Ignore Conversation to mark the articles you are not interested in.

in the *Informational Postings* articles (see page 107) often mention in their summaries that they are required reading for anyone wanting to post an article to that particular newsgroup. Take these requirements seriously if you want to be taken seriously by the group.

- Read the newsgroup's existing articles to get a feel for the kinds of issues the newsgroup deals with. If you're burning to ask a question or bring up an issue that doesn't fit the pattern, look somewhere else. Off-topic articles can provoke strident follow-ups.

- Also read the articles to make sure someone hasn't already asked your question or put your issue on the table for discussion. That means *all* the articles. Outlook Express downloads only a certain number of articles at a time (see the tip on page 111), so make sure you download and read them all.

The main point to remember is that every article you post takes up time for the newsgroup's readers and takes up disk space on the thousands of news servers that are the backbone of the newsgroup system. Tossing a casual contribution into a newsgroup as you whiz by may seem harmless enough, but why bother if you don't intend to return to see people's responses? The value of a newsgroup depends on the quality of the ideas and information exchanged over time or on the fun people have communicating electronically with each other. If you spend much time in a newsgroup, you'll find that you get out of it only as much as you put into it, and pretty soon, you'll get as irritated by casual intruders as the veteran members do.

Well, that's enough preaching. It's time to see how to post articles. In the following sections, you aren't connected to your ISP, so you can't actually post. But our descriptions will give enough information for you to be able to post your own articles later on.

Following Up on Articles

Suppose you want to follow up on the article whose text is now displayed in the bottom right pane of the Outlook Express window. Follow the steps on the facing page.

Efficient browsing
You can increase your efficiency with newsgroups by working offline as much as possible. To set up a newsgroup so that you can browse its headers offline, right-click the newsgroup in the folder list pane and choose Properties from the shortcut menu. On the Synchronize tab, first click the When Synchronizing option and then select New Headers and click OK. You then download only the headers of new articles posted to the group. Offline, you can browse through the headers, select an article of interest, and then choose Mark For Offline and Download Message Later from the Tools menu. Then connect to your ISP and choose Synchronize Newsgroup from the Tools menu to download the articles whose headers you have marked. If you want to work online, you can browse and mark headers by choosing Options from the Tools menu, clicking the Read tab, deselecting the Automatically Download Message When Viewing In The Preview Pane option, and clicking OK. To read a particular article, select its header and press the Spacebar.

The Reply To Group button

1. Click the Reply To Group button on the toolbar to display this window:

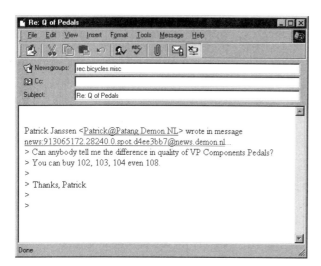

Notice that the Newsgroups and Subject boxes are already filled in. The subject is the same as that of the article you are following up on, with *Re:* added if the original article is the start of a thread. If this article has already been stored on your hard drive, or if you are connected to your ISP, the original article appears at the bottom of the message area preceded by > marks. You can edit this quoted material as appropriate.

2. For demonstration purposes, type a short, courteous reply and choose Send Later from the File menu.

Sending to the Outbox

3. If you see a dialog box commenting on the relative lengths of the article and your follow-up, click OK to send the follow-up anyway.

4. If you see a dialog box telling you that the message can be sent later from the Outbox, click OK.

The Send button

That's it! Under normal circumstances, you would be connected to your ISP and could click the Send button on the toolbar to send the follow-up on its way. As it is, Outlook Express puts the article in the Outbox, waiting for the next time you connect to the Internet.

Posting New Articles

Composing and posting new articles is similar to composing and sending e-mail messages except that you don't have to enter the address of the recipient. Follow these steps:

The New Message button

1. With the *rec.bicycles.misc* newsgroup still active in the Outlook Express window, click the New Message button to open a window with the newsgroup's name already in the Newsgroups box.

2. Type a subject, press Tab, and type an article like this one:

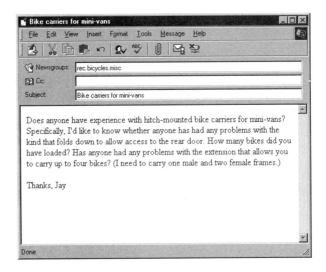

E-mailing a follow-up

Sometimes it is more appropriate to e-mail a response to the person who posted an article than it is to take up the time of newsgroup members with a follow-up, especially if the response contributes little to the general discussion. (A *thank you* note falls into this category.) You can click the Reply To Sender button to send an e-mail response. You can click the Forward button to forward an article via e-mail to a specific person.

Advertising

Commercial advertising is frowned on in most newsgroups and is likely to instigate flaming (as well as boycotts). *Spamming* (the practice of posting the same material to multiple newsgroups) is virulently opposed, not only by newsgroup members themselves but also by ISPs, who have been known to cancel the accounts of people caught in the act. Some newsgroups tolerate a simple, non-hyped announcement of a new product or service that directly relates to the members' interests. These announcements are less likely to raise hackles if they come from a seasoned member with a reputation for intelligent participation in the newsgroup; in other words, don't just drop in on a newsgroup and make an announcement. Some categories have want-ad or marketplace subcategories for personal transactions, but using these newsgroups for commercial advertising may not be well-received.

3. Because you are not connected to your ISP, choose Send Later from the File menu to simulate posting the article. (Again, you would click the Send button if you were posting a real article.)

If you were actually posting this article, it would show up in the newsgroup after a while as the beginning of a new thread. Other people's follow-ups would be given *Re:* headers and be grouped under your article to designate them as responses, whether they were posted hours or even days later.

We have one bit of tidying up to do before we end this chapter. Because you used the Send Later command, your articles are now sitting in Outlook Express's Outbox and you need to delete them:

1. Click the Outbox in the folder list pane of the Outlook Express window to display its two items in the header pane, like this:

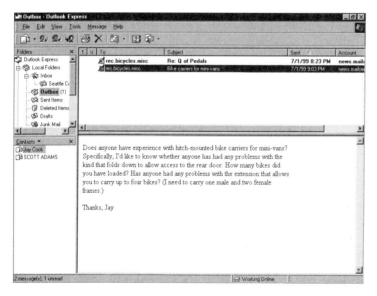

2. Select both articles and click the Delete button on the toolbar. Now there's no chance that your bogus articles will waste the time of the *rec.bicycles.misc* members.

3. Close Outlook Express.

Communicating with NetMeeting

E-mail and newsgroups aren't the only ways to communicate over the Internet. In this chapter, you learn how to use NetMeeting, which enables you to "chat," collaborate on projects, send and receive files, and hold audio and video conferences with people in distant locations.

Using techniques in this chapter, you can have productive meetings with people in different locations, whether to conduct business or catch up with friends and family.

Tasks performed and concepts covered:

Work together on one document stored on one computer

Type messages to have an electronic "conversation"

Send and receive files and programs

Draw objects on a collective whiteboard

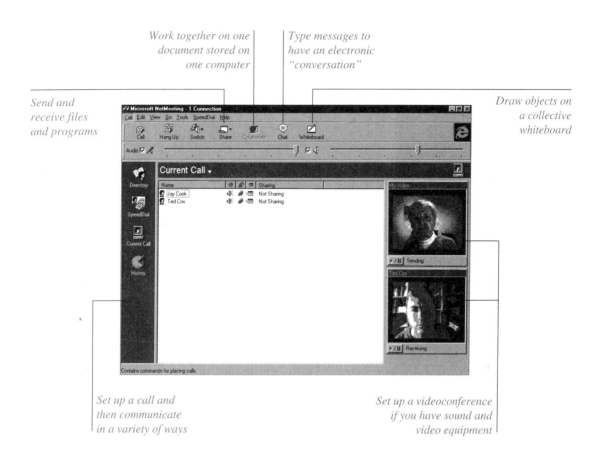

Set up a call and then communicate in a variety of ways

Set up a videoconference if you have sound and video equipment

Mastering e-mail and newsgroups is very important for efficient communication using the Internet, but with Internet Explorer 5 you can do much more than simply use e-mail to exchange short messages with colleagues and friends and use newsgroups to participate in worldwide discussions. In this chapter, you take a look at Internet communications of a different kind as you explore some of the capabilities of the Microsoft NetMeeting program.

NetMeeting supplements the written communication provided by Outlook Express with some exciting direct communication capabilities. You can *chat* with other people by typing what you want to say—they see what you type and you see what they type. And you can collaborate with others by working on a *whiteboard*—you can all see and manipulate whiteboard objects on your screens. Similarly, you can collaborate with others on documents, spreadsheets, and presentations. In addition, NetMeeting provides the technology for both spoken and visual communications. If your computer is equipped with a sound card and microphone, you can hold *audioconferences* instead of placing long-distance telephone calls; and if your computer is equipped with a video camera and a video capture card, you can hold *videoconferences*.

So how does NetMeeting work? In order to communicate with another person using NetMeeting, both of you have to log onto a *directory server* that will act as the "host" for your communication activities. (Confusingly, when you select a server to log onto, you select an *ils*, which stands for *Internet locator service*, not a *ds*.) Here's an analogy. Suppose you and a colleague arrange to meet at a local café frequented by business people to discuss a project. You can think of the directory server as the café—the venue where the communication with your colleague takes place. Before you can actually communicate, both of you have to show up at the café at a prearranged time, and you have to make contact and initiate communication. Once you have made contact, which NetMeeting refers to as *setting up a call*, you can communicate in a variety of ways, depending on the task at hand.

You could also just show up at the café, walk in, look around, find someone who might be interesting to talk to, ask if you

Directory server

Internet locator service

can join them at their table, and start talking. However, that type of communication is more likely to occur on your own time, when your goal is to while away an hour or two socializing. You would choose a directory server frequented by people who were similarly interested in engaging in friendly conversations, rather than a business-oriented server.

Setting Up NetMeeting

Before you can use NetMeeting, it must be set up on your computer. If you are responsible for this task, follow these steps:

1. Connect to your ISP and choose Programs, Internet Explorer, and then Microsoft NetMeeting from the Start menu. The Microsoft NetMeeting Wizard starts and displays its introductory dialog box:

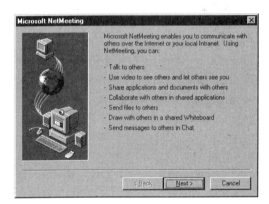

2. Click Next to go to this dialog box, which asks whether you want to log onto a directory server when you start NetMeeting:

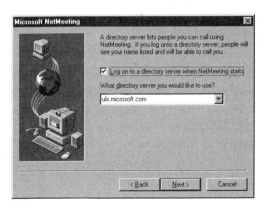

As you can see, the wizard has selected a directory server. This server will suit you for now, so click Next to move to this dialog box:

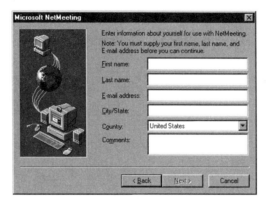

3. Enter your e-mail address and fill in any of the other boxes you want to. (This information appears in the directory listing, which lists everyone who is currently logged onto the server. You can see what everyone else enters in this dialog box and they can see what you enter, so think twice before divulging personal information.) Click Next to display this dialog box:

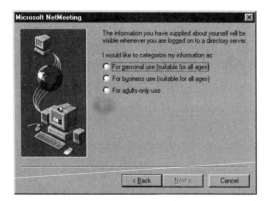

Categories of use

When you are logged onto a directory server, the list of people who are also logged on is sorted by category of use. You see all the other people who are logged on for the same purpose you are. To switch categories, select from the Category drop-down list in NetMeeting's Directory window (see page 124).

4. Select a category of use—for example, For Business Use—and click Next.

5. Select the speed of your Internet connection and click Next. The wizard displays the dialog box on the facing page.

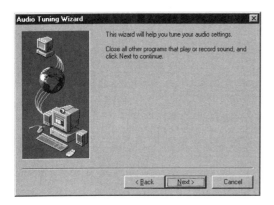

6. You need to tune your audio settings by checking your sound card and microphone. Follow the directions, clicking Next to move from one test to another. (If you don't have sound equipment on your computer, or you want to communicate with text only, follow the wizard's instructions as if you did have a sound card and microphone.) When you're done, click Finish to close the wizard and start NetMeeting.

7. If you see a message box that looks like this:

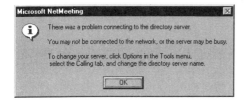

click OK and see the tip below. A NetMeeting window like the one shown at the top of the next page appears.

Problems connecting to a directory server

Sometimes when you log onto NetMeeting, you might see a message box telling you of some sort of problem connecting to the default server. You can try to access a different server by clicking the arrow at the right end of the Server box in the Directory window and selecting an option from the drop-down list. When you locate an available server, you can designate it as the one you want to log onto by choosing Options from the Tools menu, clicking the Calling tab, selecting the server from the Server Name drop-down list, and clicking OK. NetMeeting then attempts to log onto that server. The new Server Name setting remains in effect as the default until you change it again.

The directories list

You can display the list of available directory servers by clicking the arrow to the right of the Server box or by clicking the arrow to the right of the directory name in the workspace title bar. When you select a server, NetMeeting attempts to retrieve the list of people currently logged on.

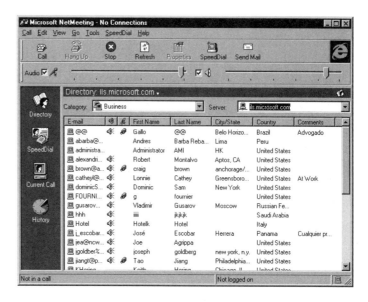

The NetMeeting window is divided into panes, with a short-cut bar on the left and the workspace on the right. At the moment, the workspace title bar tells you that the default directory is displayed in the workspace. (You'll display the contents of some of the other icons on the shortcut bar as you work your way through this chapter.) The Category box tells you that you are logged on for business purposes and the Server box tells you which directory list you are currently looking at. Below is the list of all the other people logged onto this server for this particular purpose. Anybody with a computer icon designated by a red asterisk is already involved in a call. A speaker icon indicates that the person's computer has sound equipment, and a camera icon indicates that his or her computer has video equipment.

Preparing NetMeeting to receive calls

You can tell NetMeeting to accept calls automatically by choosing Options from the Tools menu, and on the General tab, selecting the Automatically Accept Incoming Calls option. You can also tell NetMeeting you don't want to be bothered by any calls, by choosing the Do Not Disturb command from the Call menu.

8. To get ready for the next section, close NetMeeting and disconnect from your ISP.

Setting Up a Call

All NetMeeting activities take place in the context of a *call*. You set up a call to establish contact with the person you want to communicate with, and then you indicate the type of communication you are going to use. As an example, suppose you want to "talk" to a colleague using NetMeeting. Here's how you would set up the call:

1. E-mail or phone the colleague and arrange for a NetMeeting call at a specific time and on a specific directory server. For this example, you have agreed to use *ils.business.four11.com.*

2. At the designated time, connect to your ISP and start Net-Meeting.

3. Choose Options from the Tools menu and click the Calling tab to display these options:

Switching to a different server

4. Click the arrow to the right of the Server Name box, select ils.business.four11.com from the drop-down list, and click OK. NetMeeting displays this message box:

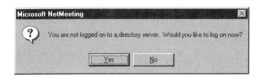

5. Click Yes. After a pause, the list in the NetMeeting window refreshes itself to display information about the other people logged onto this server.

Joining a named meeting

If you want to join a meeting that is being held on your server, click the Join The Meeting Named check box in the New Call dialog box, type the name of the meeting, and click Call. (You can also leave the edit box blank. Then when you click Call, NetMeeting will show you a list of the current meetings so that you can select the one you want.) This type of meeting might be a teleconference set up by a teleconferencing company, or an online public forum or focus group.

The Call button

6Select the e-mail address of your colleague in the E-Mail column and click the Call button on the toolbar. You see a dialog box like this one:

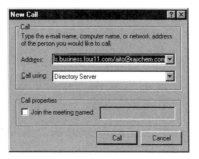

7Click Call to initiate a call request. The NetMeeting program on your computer contacts the NetMeeting program on your colleague's computer, asking whether he or she will accept the call. (This may take a while.) Once the call is accepted, the Current Call icon displays its contents in the workspace, and you see a list of the call participants, like the one shown here:

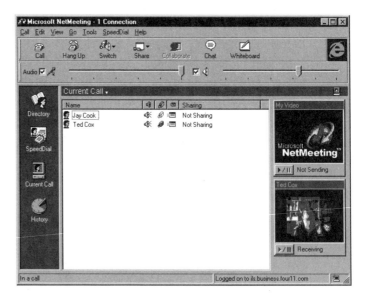

If you are on the receiving end of a call request, you see the dialog box shown at the top of the facing page.

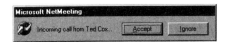

You can respond by either accepting or rejecting the call. Assuming you are expecting the request, click the Accept button. You then see the contents of the Current Call icon, as shown on the facing page.

You can now communicate with call participants in a variety of ways, which will be discussed in the next few sections. (When you are ready to end the call, you will simply click the Hang Up button on the NetMeeting toolbar.)

The Hang Up button

Chatting

Chatting is a relatively low-tech way of communicating by typing on the screen. It is popular because it's immediate, it's inexpensive, and unlike audio and videoconferencing, more than two people can get involved in the conversation.

Social chatting also offers the advantage of being anonymous. You can project a fantasy persona into cyberspace with very little risk that someone will call your bluff. Of course, the downside is that you never know whether the people you are "talking" to are also play-acting. The moral for those of you who want to use NetMeeting for socializing: have fun but be wary.

To chat with the colleague with whom you've just established a call, follow the steps on the next page.

No e-mail address?

If you don't see the e-mail address of your colleague but you know he or she is logged onto the same directory server you are, you can initiate a call by choosing New Call from the Call menu. In the Address box, type the e-mail address of your colleague and then click Call. NetMeeting initiates the call in the usual way.

NetMeeting buttons not available

Many of the NetMeeting features discussed in this chapter are available for use only if you are participating in a NetMeeting call. So if you can't find a particular button on the toolbar, it may be because you aren't yet participating in a call with at least one other NetMeeting user.

1. From the Current Call window, click the Chat button on the toolbar to display this Chat window:

Clicking the Chat button automatically opens the Chat window on your colleague's screen as well as on yours.

2. Type *When do you think you'll be finished with your review of the new specifications?* and press Enter. The message appears both on your screen and your colleague's. Here's what your screen looks like after a keyboard conversation:

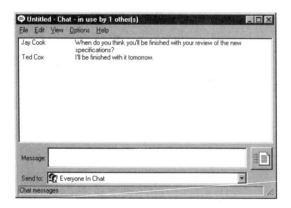

Changing the chat font

You can change the text style used in the Chat window by choosing Font from the Options menu and then selecting the font, style, and size, as well as any special effects.

Suppose the conversation involves a more lengthy and more formal discussion, and you want to keep a record of it. You also want to be able to see more text on the screen. Here's what you do:

1. Choose Clear All from the Edit menu and click No to clear the screen.

2. Choose Chat Format from the Options menu to display this dialog box:

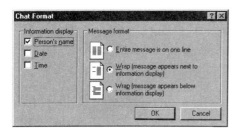

3. Click the Date and Time check boxes to add those items to the information display, select the third option in the Message Format section, and click OK.

4. Type your comments and read the comments of your colleague, which now look something like this:

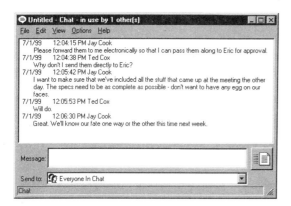

Microsoft Chat

If you want to chat with other people socially in a conventional Internet chat room, you might want to take the time to explore the Microsoft Chat program. This program has all the features of a regular chat program, but it uses a comic-strip format for your conversations. You select a cartoon character and deliver your words of wisdom in "balloons." Your character can express emotions that convey at a glance your feelings on a topic. To start Chat, choose Programs, then Internet Explorer, and then Microsoft Chat from the Start menu.

Whispering

Suppose you are participating in a call with several other people and you want to chat with only one of them. You can select that person's name from the Send To drop-down list at the bottom of the Chat window. Then when you type a message and press Enter, only that person will see what you typed.

Saving conversations

5. To record the conversation, choose Save As from the File menu, assign the chat file a name, and click Save. (From now on, you can save new versions of the same chat file by choosing the Save command.)

Printing conversations

6. If you want, print the conversation by choosing Print from the File menu.

7. Click the Chat window's Close button to end the session. If NetMeeting gives you the opportunity to save any additions to the conversation, click No.

Using the Whiteboard

Two or more call participants can work concurrently on projects by using NetMeeting's Whiteboard component. The Whiteboard is an onscreen drawing board, where you can collaboratively diagram processes, work out schedules, sketch designs, and so on. For this example, suppose you want to come to an agreement with a couple of colleagues located in distant cities about the procedure by which you will all write and produce a company report. You have already established a NetMeeting call and now you want to use the Whiteboard to diagram the procedure. Follow these steps:

The Whiteboard button

1. Click the Whiteboard button on the toolbar to display this Whiteboard window:

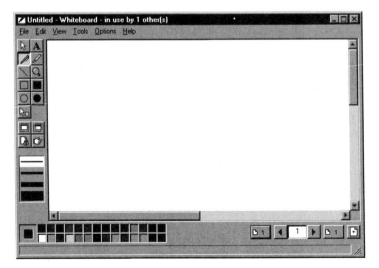

The Whiteboard automatically opens on the screens of all call participants when you send Whiteboard data to them. You can copy items from other programs and paste them on the Whiteboard from the Clipboard, or you can draw them from scratch.

2 Maximize the window and click the Unfilled Ellipse button in the toolbox on the left side of the window. Then move to the top left corner of the window, hold down the left mouse button, and drag to draw a skinny oval.

The Unfilled Ellipse button

3 Click the Text button, click an insertion point at the left end of the oval, and type *Write* and your initials.

The Text button

4 Continue to collaboratively draw ovals and lines to create a diagram that looks something like this:

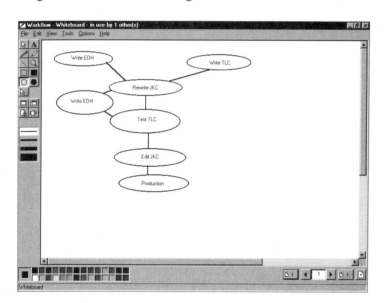

You can zoom in or out by choosing Zoom from the View menu or by clicking the Zoom button.

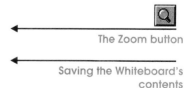

The Zoom button

5 When you've finished, save the contents of the Whiteboard by choosing the Save As command from the File menu, assigning a filename, and clicking Save.

Saving the Whiteboard's contents

Suppose you have been working on the masthead for your Web site and you want your colleagues' opinions about the current design. Follow these steps to see how you might use the Whiteboard to get their feedback:

1. Display the taskbar and click the Launch Internet Explorer button. Then *type www.quickcourse.com* in the Address bar and press Enter to move to that Web site.

2. Click the Whiteboard button on the taskbar to switch back to the Whiteboard, and choose New from the File menu. Click Yes when NetMeeting asks you to confirm that you want to discard the current Whiteboard page.

The Select Area button

3. Click the Select Area button in the toolbox, and if NetMeeting displays a message telling you to select an area on the screen, click OK. NetMeeting then jumps to the screen that was displayed before the Whiteboard—in this case the Quick Course home page.

4. Drag a selection rectangle around the graphic banner at the top of the page. NetMeeting jumps back to the Whiteboard and inserts the image within the selection rectangle on the Whiteboard page, like this:

5. Now click the Remote Pointer On button to display a pointing hand icon and drag the icon to the Catalog graphic. Then click the Text button, click an insertion point below the hand icon, and type *I've used a book icon here. OK?* The results are shown below:

The Remote Pointer On button

If you want, you can print a paper copy of the Whiteboard window's contents by choosing the Print command.

6. Experiment with some of the other Whiteboard tools and commands. Then when you're ready, close its window, clicking No to discard the Whiteboard contents.

7. Close Internet Explorer and if necessary, click the NetMeeting button on the taskbar to reactivate its window.

Collaborating on Projects

Suppose you are working on a document and would like input from your colleagues. NetMeeting enables you to collaborate on such projects at two levels:

• **View only.** The owner of the document can share it with participants in a NetMeeting call in such a way that they can see the document but cannot work on it.

Collaborate with caution

When you collaborate with someone using NetMeeting, you are in effect giving that person access to your computer and its files. Obviously, you should be cautious about the people with whom you collaborate. If you share a Windows Explorer window, you share all windows that you open during that session, including any applications that you start while participating in the call. Sharing a folder on your computer shares all the subfolders, files, and documents contained in that folder.

- **Change**The owner can give other call participants access to the document so that they can make changes to it.

Because not all of you will have the same file on your computers, we'll go through the steps for both levels of collaboration using a hypothetical example. (If you want, you can follow along with these steps with your own file, extrapolating from our instructions as necessary.) Suppose you and a couple of colleagues who are located in an office across town are developing a modest Web site for use as an information resource on your organization's intranet. You have taken a first stab at creating the Web site using Microsoft FrontPage Express. (See the adjacent tip for more information.) Here's how you might all collaborate on this project, in spite of the physical distance between you:

Using FrontPage Express

As you explore the World Wide Web, you inevitably get ideas about ways you could use a Web site to communicate with potential customers about a product line, with existing customers about product availability and support, with colleagues about areas of professional interest, and so on. If all you need is a simple, relatively static site that conveys the necessary information without much hoopla, you can take advantage of Microsoft FrontPage Express, a stripped-down version of Microsoft's FrontPage Web authoring program, which is included with Internet Explorer. FrontPage Express enables you to design a Web page while viewing the results as they will appear in Internet Explorer. You no longer have to learn HTML coding to put together a decent-looking Web page. If nothing else, playing around with FrontPage will give you a feel for how Web sites are created and an appreciation for some of the more design-intensive sites you'll encounter on your Web excursions.

1 First contact your colleagues and tell them that you will be hosting a meeting (a call) on your computer at 1:15 PM to enlist their help in refining a page of the Web site. Make sure they know your e-mail address and the directory server you will be using.

2 A few minutes before the specified time, connect to your ISP and start Internet Explorer. Then start NetMeeting and log onto the specified directory. Your colleagues do the same.

3 Choose Host Meeting from the Call menu. If this is the first time you have hosted a meeting, you see this dialog box:

4 Click OK.

5 Your colleagues ask to join the meeting by clicking the SpeedDial icon, double-clicking your entry in the SpeedDial window, and specifying that they want to join your meeting. (See the tip on the facing page for information about SpeedDial.) Accept their requests. Their names join yours on the Current Call tab of everyone's NetMeeting window.

6. Display the taskbar, and click the Start button. Choose Internet Explorer and Microsoft FrontPage Express from the Programs submenu, and open the Web site on your computer.

7. Switch to NetMeeting, click the Share button on the NetMeeting toolbar, and select FrontPage Express from the drop-down list. NetMeeting displays this dialog box:

The Share button

8. Click OK, minimize the NetMeeting window, and begin to work on the Web site. The call participants watch you work on the document, which appears in a window on their screens. They can't make any changes to the document, but they can send their comments and suggestions to you by using Chat.

9. To let your colleagues make changes to the Web page, switch to NetMeeting and click the Collaborate button on the NetMeeting toolbar. NetMeeting displays this dialog box:

The Collaborate button

SpeedDial

By default, NetMeeting adds people you call and who call you to a list displayed in the workspace when you click the SpeedDial icon. Double-click a name in the SpeedDial list to request a call with that person. You can send your SpeedDial information to someone by clicking the SpeedDial button on NetMeeting's toolbar, filling in the edit boxes, clicking Send To Mail Recipient, and clicking OK. (You can also use this dialog box to manually add a SpeedDial entry to your list.) In the New Message window, enter the recipient's address and a subject, and send the message.

Sorting the directory list

Sort the directory list on any column by clicking its header. For example, click the E-mail column header once to sort it alphabetically and click it again to reverse the sort order. Click the Audio or Video column header to group all the listings with audio or video.

10. Click OK and switch back to FrontPage Express. If one of your colleagues wants to take part in this collaborative endeavor, he or she also clicks the Collaborate button, then clicks the left mouse button to take control of the cursor, and edits and formats the active document in the usual way. (Obviously, only one person can edit the document at a time.)

11. When everyone is satisfied, take control of the Web page by clicking the mouse button and stop the collaboration by switching back to NetMeeting and clicking the Collaborate button again to deselect it. Then click OK.

12. Close FrontPage Express, saving the active Web page as a file in your My Documents folder.

You could then end the meeting by clicking the Hang Up button on the NetMeeting toolbar, but don't do that yet.

Sending and Receiving Files

As well as actively collaborating on files, you can use NetMeeting's file sharing feature to send and receive files. Suppose that before terminating the call with your colleagues, you decide everyone should have a copy of the Web page you all worked on. Here's how to send the file:

1. Choose File Transfer and then Send File from the Tools menu. In the Select A File To Send dialog box, navigate to the My Documents folder. The dialog box looks like this:

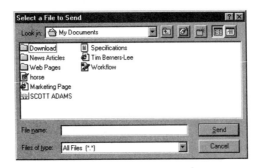

Sending to one person

To send a file to only one of several call participants, right-click that person's name in the Current Call list and choose Send File from the shortcut menu. Then in the Open File dialog box, locate and double-click the file to start the transfer.

2. Select the file you want to transfer and click Send.

3. When you see a message telling you the transfer was completed successfully, click OK.

If you are on the receiving end of a file transfer, you see this dialog box when the transfer is complete:

You can then make a note of the name of the file and click Close. It will be stored in the C:\Program Files\NetMeeting\Received Files folder.

Audioconferencing and Videoconferencing

Provided you have the necessary audio equipment, you can start a NetMeeting call and then carry on a conversation with one other audio-equipped participant by talking into a microphone and listening to responses over your speakers. And if you have the necessary video equipment, you can send and receive video images. Put the two together, and you can hold videoconferences (but the success of this experience will depend a lot on your equipment and server traffic). Here's how:

1. Assuming you have started NetMeeting and are logged onto an agreed-upon directory server, locate the e-mail address of your colleague and request a call.

2. When the call is accepted, make sure that check marks appear in the microphone and speaker check boxes on the Audio toolbar. Then test the volume of your microphone and speakers with a few words of greeting. Make any necessary adjustments using the two volume control bars. (You can mute the microphone or the speakers by deselecting their check boxes.)

   ← Audioconferencing

3. Say what you need to say.

4. End the audio session (but not the call) by clicking the speaker icon next to the name of the person you are talking to and choosing Stop Using Audio And Video from the shortcut menu.

5. Finally, end the call by clicking the Hang Up button on the NetMeeting toolbar.

Now try sending and receiving video images. You can send video images to a call participant who does not have video equipment attached to his or her computer, and you can receive images whether or not you have video equipment. However, this example assumes that both you and your colleague have the necessary cameras and video capture boards and that you're trying out this new means of communication. Try this:

Videoconferencing → 1. After logging onto a directory server but before setting up a call, choose Options from the Tools menu and click the Video tab to display this dialog box:

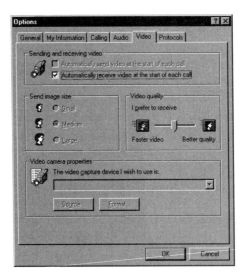

2. Select both the Automatically Send Video and Automatically Receive Video check boxes and click OK. (If your computer has no video equipment, the Automatically Send Video check box is unavailable.)

3. In the directory listing in the NetMeeting window, find the e-mail address of the person with whom you want to exchange video data and request a call. When the call is accepted, the

What do you look like?
If you want to check what you will look like to the person receiving your video image before you establish the call, click the button at the bottom of the My Video window. Check the lighting, your position in relation to the camera, and so on. When you're satisfied, place the call and proceed with the video-conference.

contents of the Current Call icon are shown in the workspace. Assuming that both of you have selected the Automatically Receive Video and Automatically Send Video options, you can now see your colleague (or whatever images he or she is sending you) in the Remote Video window, as shown below:

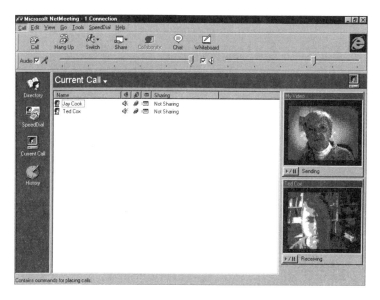

4. To end the video session, click the camera icon next to the name of the person you are communicating with and choose Stop Using Audio And Video from the shortcut menu.

5. End the call by clicking the Hang Up button on the toolbar.

You can start a call with several people and then talk to each in turn, or send video images to each in turn. Click the Switch button on the toolbar, select the name of the first person you want to communicate with, and talk and/or send video. Then click the Switch button, click the name of the second person, and talk and/or send video. And so on. While you are talking or sending video to one call participant, two other call participants can also be talking or sending video.

This has been a very quick overview of NetMeeting's capabilities—nothing more than a teaser, really. But if you frequently need to communicate with distant colleagues more directly than you can with e-mail (or regular mail), you might want to explore NetMeeting's capabilities further.

The Switch button

Video on demand

To control when you send and receive video, deselect both the Automatically Send Video and the Automatically Receive Video options on the Video tab of the Options dialog box. Then click the buttons at the bottom of the My Video and Remote Video windows to initiate the sending and receiving of video images.

Customizing
Internet Explorer

You customize the program window and adjust the display speed. Then we show you how to change Internet Explorer's starting page and how to access the Web directly from the desktop. Finally, you fine-tune Internet Explorer's security features.

The techniques discussed in this chapter increase the efficiency and security with which you can work with the Internet, so that you can focus on your particular interests and needs.

Tasks performed and concepts covered:

Display all the tools you need to explore the Web on a single row

Use fullscreen view to devote as much space as possible to Web sites

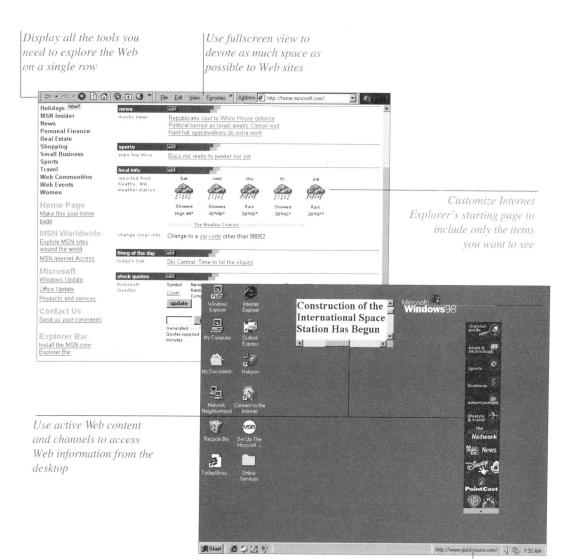

Customize Internet Explorer's starting page to include only the items you want to see

Use active Web content and channels to access Web information from the desktop

Add Web-site toolbars to the taskbar for instant access at any time

Internet Explorer's default settings control the way the program looks on the screen and, to a certain extent, the way Web sites appear in the viewing area. You can change these settings at any time, and in the first part of this chapter, you learn how to customize Internet Explorer to suit the way you work. Then you move on to more sophisticated customization. You personalize Internet Explorer's default starting page and then switch to a different starting page so that the information you use the most is displayed when the program opens. Then you look at ways to make the information you want to see easily accessible even when you are not running Internet Explorer. Finally, you fine-tune Internet Explorer's security features to take care of some of the safety issues discussed in this book's Introduction (see page xiii).

Customizing the Display

You can tailor the display to meet your needs in a variety of ways. Customizing some of the features puts your own decorative stamp on Internet Explorer's interface (its way of presenting information). Customizing others, like the first set of items discussed here, can have an impact on your working efficiency.

Enlarging the Viewing Area

In Chapter 1, we showed you how to adjust the components of the Internet Explorer window to enlarge the space available for viewing Web pages (see page 18). This basic configuration may suit the way you work, and you may not be interested in learning about more ways to set up your screen. However, there are one or two other adjustment you can make to give Web pages a little more elbow room on the screen.

Turning Off Screen Elements

Different people work in different ways. In Chapter 1, you shrank the size of the Standard toolbar by turning off text labels and displaying small icons, but suppose you prefer to choose commands from menus and would just as soon dispense with the toolbar completely. Follow these steps:

1.   Without connecting to your ISP, start Internet Explorer.

2. Right-click anywhere on the toolbar and choose Standard
   Buttons from the shortcut menu to turn it off. (You can also
   turn off the toolbar by choosing Toolbars and then Standard
   Buttons from the View menu.)

Turning off window
components

3. Now how do you perform the tasks assigned to the hidden
   buttons? Choose Go To from the View menu to display this
   submenu:

As you can see, some buttons are represented on the View
menu as commands, including the Stop and Refresh buttons.
Still more buttons have equivalent commands on the Go To
submenu, including the Back, Forward, and Home buttons.

4. Move the pointer to the Explorer Bar command to see a submenu that includes these commands:

Here you'll find the equivalents of the Search, Favorites, and
History buttons. Commands for the other two buttons on the
Standard toolbar, Print and Edit With Microsoft FrontPage
Editor, are located on the File menu.

5. Choose Toolbars and then Address Bar from the View menu
   to turn off the Address bar.

Turning off the Address bar

6. Now how do you enter a URL to move to a different Web site?
   Choose Open from the File menu to display the dialog box
   shown on the next page.

Opening URLs

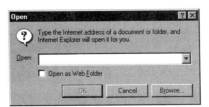

Cached sites ──────────▶

7. Type *www.yahoo.com* in the Open edit box and press Enter to jump to Yahoo's Web site. (This site should be stored, or *cached*, on your hard drive and should be available even though you are working offline. If Internet Explorer wants to go online to find the Yahoo site, tell the program not to bother and continue working offline.)

Now suppose you frequently use the Explorer bar to get from place to place. With your new window configuration, the Explorer bar options are just a menu-command away. Try this:

1. Choose Explorer Bar and then History from the View menu to open the Explorer bar so that you can access Web pages you've recently visited.

Changing the History list view ──────────▶

2. Point to the View button at the top of the Explorer bar and select By Most Visited. Your screen looks something like this:

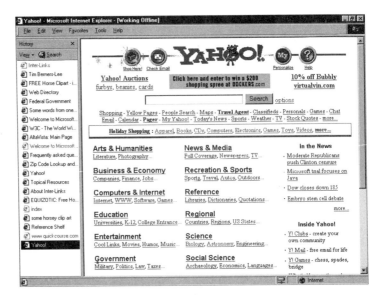

3. Click Search. In the Search For edit box, type Inter-Links and click Search Now. Immediately, Internet Explorer filters out the pages in your history list that belong to the Inter-Links Web site.

← Searching the History list

4. Click the Close button (the X) on the History title bar to close the Explorer bar.

   Using commands instead of the toolbar and Address bar involves a few extra steps. Let's look at another way of keeping everything at hand without taking up screen "real estate."

Switching to Fullscreen View

You can decrease the amount of space consumed by the program window by using Internet Explorer's fullscreen view. Follow these steps:

1. Choose Fullscreen from the View menu. (You can also press the F11 key.) Here's the result:

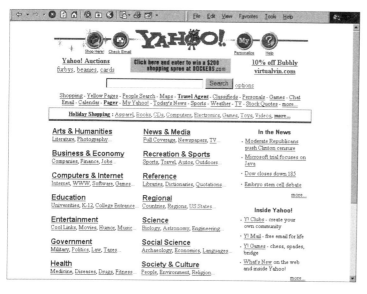

Internet Explorer has turned off both the status bar and the title bar, and has moved the Standard toolbar and the menu bar into the space formerly occupied by the title bar at the top of the screen.

Changing the font size

Another way to get more text on the screen is to shrink the size of the font used to display Web pages. (The font sizes are generally defined by the pages' designers to achieve a desired effect, but usually Internet Explorer can override the designers' specifications.) Choose Text size from the View menu to display a submenu of relative sizes, and choose either Smaller or Smallest to reduce the size of the font.

2. Right-click the toolbar or menu bar and choose Address Bar from the shortcut menu. Then right-click the Address Bar and choose Go Button to toggle off the button.

3. Drag the move handles (the gray bars) at the left end of the menu bar and the Address bar to the left until the row of tools at the top of the screen looks like this:

With this configuration, you can easily access the buttons, commands, and Web sites you use most often. To use a hidden button or command, click the More Buttons or More Commands button at the right end of the toolbar or menu bar.

Want even more space? Try this:

Hiding the row of tools

1. Choose Toolbars and then Auto Hide from the View menu. The row of tools disappears, and your screen looks like this:

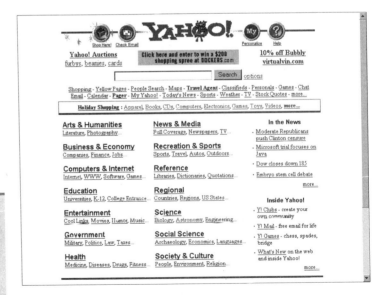

Turning off the menu bar

If you find you seldom use the commands on Internet Explorer's menus, you can turn off the menu bar to gain screen space. Right-click the menu bar, a toolbar, or the Address bar and then choose Menu Bar from the shortcut menu to toggle it off.

2. Point to the top of the screen. The row of tools reappears, just as the autohidden Windows taskbar does when you point to the bottom of the screen.

3. Choose Toolbars and then Auto Hide from the View menu to redisplay the row of tools.

You'll work in fullscreen view for the remainder of this chapter, but don't be afraid to experiment with your screen configuration. Changes you make to the program window remain in effect only until you change them again. You can always come back later and reset these options any way you want them.

Speeding Up Page Display

Heavy traffic on the Web can slow you down just like heavy highway traffic can. Animation, video clips, sound, and pictures all give Web pages pizazz, but they can take forever to download. One simple way to speed up page display is to tell Internet Explorer not to bother with these elements. As a demonstration, let's visit a multimedia site and test its download speed both with and without its multimedia components:

1. Choose Work Offline from the File menu to deselect it. If necessary, click the Refresh button and when prompted, connect to your ISP.

The Refresh button

2. Open the CNN Interactive page at *www.cnn.com* by choosing it from the Daily News folder of your Favorites list.

3. Before Internet Explorer has fully downloaded the page, click any hyperlink to move on. Notice that you don't have to wait until everything is in place to get on with your work.

It doesn't take more than a couple of visits to graphic-rich Web sites like CNN Interactive to figure out that, although they are attractive, downloading them can be slow. Suppose all you want to do is get in, glance at the news headlines, and move on. Follow these steps to tell Internet Explorer to block some of the slower components:

1. Click the menu bar's More Commands button to display a drop-down list of hidden menus. Then click Tools and choose Internet Options from the submenu. Click the Advanced tab to display the options shown on the next page.

Stopping in mid-access

If you grow impatient while waiting for Internet Explorer to display a Web page, you can always click the Stop button on the Standard toolbar to abort the downloading process. If that toolbar is not displayed, you can choose Stop from the View menu or press the Esc key.

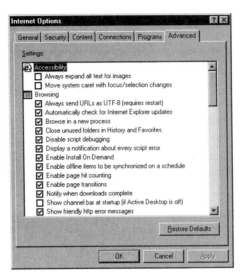

Turning off graphics

2. Scroll down to the Multimedia category, deselect the Show Pictures check box, and click OK.

3. Now move to the New York Times page at *www.nytimes.com*. Notice the graphic placeholder frames, which look something like this:

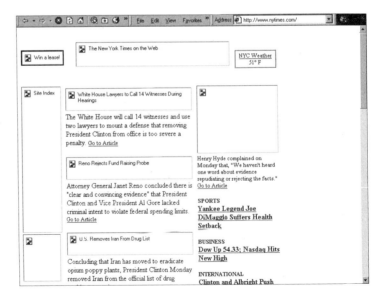

4. Right-click a placeholder and choose Show Picture from the shortcut menu to display only that graphic. All the other graphics still have placeholders.

Displaying a specific graphic

5. Return to the Advanced tab of the Internet Options dialog box, select the Show Pictures check box, and click OK.

6. Choose Refresh from the View menu. (You can also press the F5 key.) Graphics appear in place of the placeholders.

Personalizing Internet Explorer's Default Starting Page

As you saw in Chapter 2, Internet Explorer provides many avenues for accessing information. However, one of the most efficient ways of quickly reaching the information you need is to personalize Internet Explorer's default starting page so that it includes links to the Web sites you visit regularly. In this example, the goal is to keep things as simple as possible so that you can get in and out quickly without having to wade through a lot of extraneous information. Follow these steps:

1. Click the Home button to move to the starting page.

2. Next click the *Personalize* hyperlink to display this page:

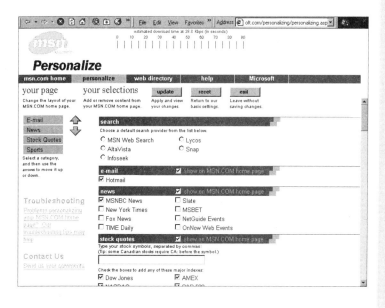

Increasing temporary storage space

As you view Web pages, Internet Explorer stores them as files in a folder on your hard drive. The next time you want to see a page you have already viewed, the program can display the page quicker because it can access the folder on your hard drive faster than it can the Web. However, the folder is allowed to grow only to a specified size, at which point, older pages are discarded. You can speed up the display of pages you visit often by increasing the folder's maximum size. Choose Internet Options from the Tools menu and click the Settings button in the Temporary Internet Files section of the General tab. Drag the Amount Of Disk Space To Use slider to the right and click OK twice. Conversely, if your hard drive is nearly full, you can decrease the space used by dragging the slider to the left. From the Internet Options dialog box, you can also adjust the amount of time the History folder keeps page links.

In the Your Selections column, you indicate which news and information sources you want on the starting page by clicking the Show On MSN.COM Home Page check box to turn it on and then selecting one or more of the category's options.

3. Click AltaVista in the Search category.

4. Deselect the Show check box in the E-Mail category.

5. Leave the News category set to show MSNBC News.

6. Deselect the Show check box for Stock Quotes, select only ESPN Top Story in the Sports category, and skip the Sports Scoreboard.

7. In the Local Info category, enter your zip code or location and select only Local Weather Forecast.

8. Bypass the remaining sections until you get to Thing Of The Day, and then select Today's Link.

Updating the page

9. Click the Update button to apply your selections to the starting page, which now looks like this:

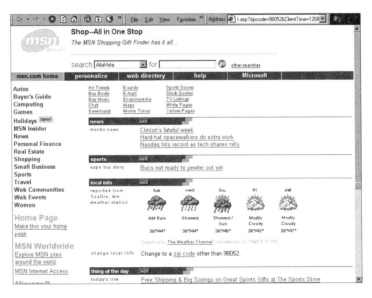

Suppose you decide that receiving stock-quote information could be useful to your work. Follow these steps to change your personalized starting page:

1. Click the *Personalize* hyperlink to jump back to the Personalize page.

2. Scroll to the Stock Quotes section, click its Show check box, and then select only NASDAQ.

3. Click the Update hyperlink.

4. Scroll to the newly added Stock Quotes section.

   To make this link even more useful, let's add a specific stock to the Get Quote box:

1. Click the *Find Symbol* hyperlink to open a page at the MSN Investor Web site:

Finding a stock symbol

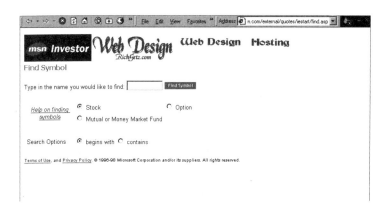

2. Type the name of a public company in the edit box and then click Find Symbol. For example, we entered *Microsoft*, and got these results:

Displaying the stock's price

3. Click the Back button twice to return to your starting page, type the stock symbol in the Get Quote box, and click the Get Quote button. Internet Explorer jumps to the MSN Investor Web site and displays the latest data on the stock, shown here:

4. After reviewing the information, click the Back button.

You can come back at any time and change the settings of your personalized starting page. For example, if you find a Web site to which you would like to have one-click access, you can scroll to the Your Links section on the Personalize page, click the Show On MSN.COM Home Page check box, and enter the site's URL and name. When you update your starting page, the link will be there, ready for you to use.

Switching the Home Page

As you have seen, by default Internet Explorer's starting page is the home page of MSN.com, Microsoft's online information service. Although Microsoft takes advantage of your visits to this page to push its products, it also provides enough Web services, plus headline news, to make this default acceptable to a good many Internet Explorer users. But suppose your company has its own Web site and you want to check out the latest corporate announcements each time you log onto the Internet. Or suppose you want to check the calendar of today's events on your school's Web site. Because you can add the MSN.com home page to your favorites list and easily access its services that way, it may make sense to change Internet Explorer's default starting page.

Suppose you decide to make your home page the Inter-Links Web site, which you used in Chapter 2 as a springboard for finding information on the Web (see page 43). Follow these steps to change Internet Explorer's starting page so that the Inter-Links home page is displayed whenever you start the program or whenever you click the Home button on the toolbar:

1. Move to the Inter-Links site by selecting it from the History list (see page 50), selecting it from the Address bar's drop-down list, or typing *http://alabanza.com/kabacoff/Inter-Links/* in the Address bar.

2. Choose Internet Options from the Tools menu to display this dialog box:

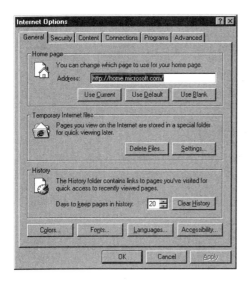

3. In the Home Page section of the General tab, click Use Current and then click OK.

Now for the acid test:

1. Close Internet Explorer.

2. Start Internet Explorer again. After a few seconds, you see the Inter-Links home page on your screen.

3. Click the Home button or choose Go To and then Home Page from the View menu. Internet Explorer reloads the Inter-Links home page.

Starting with a blank "page"

If you don't want to check a particular Web site every time you start Internet Explorer, you can open the program with a blank viewing area so that you don't have to wait for the home page to load. In the Internet Options dialog box, click the Use Blank button in the Home Page section and click OK. The next time you start Internet Explorer, you will see only a blank page.

You can now use the hyperlinks on this page or open another Web site using any of the methods we covered in Chapter 2.

Integrating the Web with the Desktop

The Internet has grown so big so fast that the amount of information available is overwhelming. To solve the problem of information overload, suppose you have decided to focus on just a few sources that you can rely on to deliver the information you need when you need it, with the least investment of your own time and effort. You want to customize your computer so that the information comes to you automatically; you don't want to go hunting for it all the time. In the next few sections, you explore a few ways to put the power of the Web at your fingertips even when you are not actively running Internet Explorer.

Active Desktop

If you are using Internet Explorer 5 with the Active Desktop, you can bring the Web right to your desktop. In Chapter 1, you saw some of the features of the Active Desktop that are available when you switch to the Web-style environment, but you stopped short of seeing its most exciting capabilities, which allow you to customize your computer to provide constant access to specified Web sites. (If you don't have Active Desktop, you will not be able to add active Web content to your desktop, but you might want to read that section anyway to get an idea of what you might be able to do if you upgraded your Windows operating system.)

Automatically Downloading Web Sites

First let's see how to synchronize Web sites so that you can view their most recent information offline. When we showed you how to create favorites in Chapter 2 (see page 49), we said we would cover the Make Available Offline option in the Add Favorite dialog box later. Let's now revisit that dialog box and see what offline browsing is all about:

Weather information

1. With your connection to your ISP active and Internet Explorer running, type *www.weather.com* in the Address bar and press

Enter. Then type your city in the Enter A City or Zip edit box and click the Go button. Internet Explorer displays a Web page like the one shown here for Seattle:

2. Choose Add To Favorites from the Favorites menu to display the dialog box shown earlier on page 49.

3. Click the Make Available Offline check box, and then start the Offline Synchronization Wizard by clicking the Customize button.

4. Click Next to move through the wizard's dialog boxes, entering the requested information. (For now, accept the defaults in each dialog.) Click Finish to close the wizard, and then click OK to add the subscribed site to your favorites list. Internet Explorer then synchronizes the Weather Channel site for the first time.

Now suppose you decide you want the day's weather delivered to your computer every morning. Here's how to change the synchronization settings:

1. Choose Synchronize from the Tools menu to display the dialog box shown on the following page.

Why browse offline?

There may be times when you know it won't be convenient—or possible—for you to connect to the Internet, but you will have the time to read Web information. When you synchronize the Web pages containing information that changes frequently (for example, weather or stock information), Internet Explorer automatically downloads the most recent information to your computer so that you can look it over later without connecting to the Internet.

2. Select The Weather Channel, click Properties, and then click the Schedule tab to display these options:

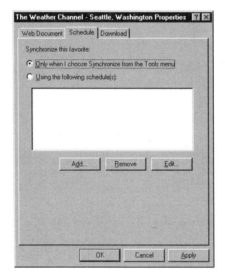

Automatically connecting for synchronization

You can set your computer to automatically connect to the Internet in order to gather the most recent information from any Web page that is synchronized. Choose Synchronize from the Tools menu, select the page you want Internet Explorer to automatically download, and click Properties. Click the Schedule tab, select Using The Following Schedule, and click the Edit button. Then click the Synchronization Items tab and select the check box that controls automatic connection.

3. Click the Using The Following Schedule(s) option, and then click the Add button to show this New Schedule dialog box:

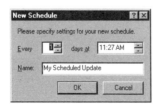

4. Change the time to the right of Days At to 9:00 AM and type *Daily at 9* in the Name box. Then click OK twice.

5. Finally, close the Items To Synchronize dialog box.

Now every morning at 9:00, Internet Explorer will download the weather report ready for you to read offline. (Obviously, your computer must be turned on and Internet Explorer must be running for the transfer to take place.) You know when the report has been updated because a red asterisk appears with the site's icon on your Favorites list. Choosing The Weather Channel from the Favorites list displays the updated Web site.

Internet Explorer can also notify you every time a synchronized page changes. Here's how to set up notification:

1. Choose Synchronize from the Tools menu.   ◄—————— Receiving notification
                                                                                                                           of changes

2. Select The Weather Channel and click Properties.

3. Click the Download tab to display these options:

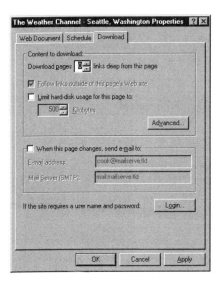

4. Click the When This Page Changes, Send E-mail To check box, enter your e-mail address and mail server address, and click OK. Then click Close.

Now Internet Explorer will periodically check this site, alerting you if it changes.

Using Channels

You can take another step into the world of automated Web surfing by using channels. Here's how to display the Channel bar and work with it directly on the desktop:

1. Close Internet Explorer.

Turning on Active Desktop

2. Right-click the desktop and choose Active Desktop and then View As Web Page from the shortcut menu. Your desktop now looks something like this:

Quick channel access

You can quickly access channels when Internet Explorer is not displayed by choosing Favorites, then Channels, then a channel category, and then a specific channel from the Start menu. If you choose Channel Guide, Internet Explorer automatically connects to the MSN.COM Web Events page.

PointCast

The PointCast channel provides access to one of the pioneers of Web-casting technology. Billed as a *free business news service*, PointCast is a customizable compilation of headlines from a variety of sources, providing up-to-date business news from around the world. The service is advertiser-supported (no fee), so be prepared for the commercials. But if a one-stop business news source is what you're looking for, you might want to take the PointCast channel for a test drive. Click PointCast on the Channel bar to open Internet Explorer with the PointCast Registration page displayed. Click Activate Now and follow the instructions to subscribe using the Setup Wizard.

3. Click any of the channel buttons to open Internet Explorer and display all the channels available for that category. For example, click News & Technology to see these icons:

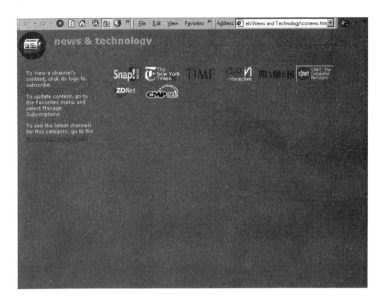

Clicking one of the icons displays a preview page for that channel, which includes a button you can click to subscribe to the channel. (The button may be labeled *Add Channel* or *Add Active Channel*.) Clicking the button updates the channel's information and starts the Offline Favorite Wizard. When you complete the wizard's dialog boxes and click Finish, Internet Explorer adds the channel to the Items To Synchronize dialog box. You can then either accept the default synchronization schedule for that channel or you can customize it (see page 156). Some channels have very aggressive synchronization schedules. For example, CNN Interactive is updated every 30 minutes, 24 hours a day. So you might want to check the default schedule to make sure it won't decrease your efficiency.

4. Close Internet Explorer and then investigate other channel categories.

Adding Web Content to the Desktop

The concept of adding Web content to the desktop is not hard to grasp, but different people will take advantage of it in different ways. In this section, you'll learn a couple of techniques that will enable you to decide how to use Web content to make your daily work easier. As an example, suppose you have a Web site you refer to often and you want to keep it close at hand. You can add Web content to the taskbar by following these steps:

Putting items on the taskbar

1. Point to the bottom of the screen to display the Windows taskbar, and right-click it. Choose Toolbars and then New Toolbar from the shortcut menu to display this dialog box:

2. Type *http://www.quickcourse.com* in the edit box, and click OK. Now the taskbar looks like this:

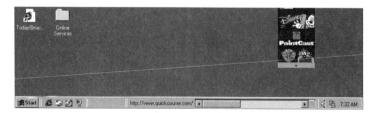

Sizing the taskbar

If you want to add several new Web-site toolbars to the taskbar but can't fit them all in, you can point to the top border of the taskbar and drag upward to create a "double-decker" taskbar. You can then try arranging all your Web-site toolbars on one deck, while retaining the other deck for program buttons.

3. Point to the move handle at the left end of the Quick Course toolbar and drag to the right until all you can see of the toolbar is its name.

4. To display the Quick Course home page, simply right-click its toolbar and choose Open In Window from the shortcut

menu. Internet Explorer starts with the page in the viewing area. Click the Close button to close the program.

If your taskbar tends to get crowded, you might want to put the Web link directly on the desktop instead. Try this:

1. Right-click the desktop, choose Properties from the shortcut menu, and click the Web tab to display these options:

Putting items on the desktop

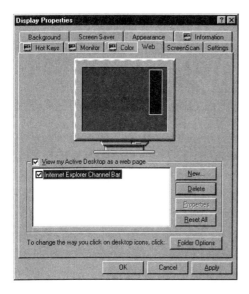

The tabs you see in the Display Properties dialog box reflect the capabilities of your video adapter and monitor, and may be different from ours.

2. Click the New button. When Internet Explorer asks whether you want to select an item from the Active Desktop gallery (see the adjacent tip), click No.

3. Click the Browse button, and then double-click NASA Homepage in your list of favorites to return to the New Active Desktop Item dialog box with that page's URL in the Location edit box. Click OK to close the dialog box and OK again to add the item to your desktop without specifying a password.

4. After Internet Explorer synchronizes the site, click OK to close the Properties dialog box.

The Active Desktop gallery

To make it easier to add items to your desktop, Microsoft maintains the Active Desktop gallery, a collection of Web sites that are likely candidates for active items. You access the gallery by clicking Yes in the New Active Desktop Item message box (displayed in the adjacent step 2). Internet Explorer starts and takes you to the Active Desktop Items page of the Microsoft Windows Media Showcase site. You can then look for items that meet your needs, display previews, and add any items you like to your desktop.

5. Back on your desktop, use the vertical scroll bar to scroll the NASA home page until you can see the headline of the main story. Then size the active item by dragging its frame until only the headline is visible. Finally, point to the top of the item to display a "title bar" and drag the bar to move the item to the top of the screen, where it looks like the one shown below. As you can see here, you now have an easy way to get the latest space exploration information directly from your desktop:

Active items on your desktop might slow down your computer somewhat, so you will delete these two items for now (you can always experiment later):

Deleting Active Desktop items

1. Right-click the taskbar and turn off your custom toolbar by choosing Toolbars and then http://www.quickcourse.com.

2. Right-click the desktop, choose Properties, click the Web tab, deselect the NASA Homepage check box, and click OK.

You might think that putting items on the desktop would be inconvenient because the desktop is often covered up by whatever application you are working with. But when you have the Quick Launch toolbar displayed on the taskbar, a simple click of the Show Desktop button minimizes all active windows and reveals the desktop. So experiment as much as you like with adding active content to your desktop.

The Show Desktop button

Customizing for Security

In the Introduction to this book, we discussed various aspects of Internet security and mentioned that Internet Explorer provides several mechanisms for protecting against the relatively small risks you take when using the Internet. In this section, we'll show you how to customize Internet Explorer to give you some peace of mind.

Managing Cookies

You'll recall from the discussion in the Introduction that a cookie is a file sent to your computer's hard drive by a Web site so that the file can store information about you and your activities on that site (see page xiii). When you visit that site again, the cookie file is checked by a program on the site's server to see what you did the last time you visited. The cookie might be used only to develop site demographics, or it could be used as a basis for tailoring your visits. For example, when you enter the site's URL, the site could automatically display the page where you spend most of your time, instead of its home page.

By default, Internet Explorer allows Web sites to store their cookies on your computer's hard drive. But the whole idea of little programs working stealthily behind the scenes to gather information about habits and preferences, no matter how innocuous or limited the information, gives some people the heebie-jeebies. If you are one of those people, you can tell Internet Explorer not to accept any cookies. Alternatively, you can specify that you want to approve all cookies before they are accepted. As a demonstration, here are the steps for setting up cookie approval:

1. Start Internet Explorer, choose Internet Options from the Tools menu, and click the Security tab. Then with Internet selected, click the Custom Level button and scroll the Settings list to the Cookies section, which looks like this:

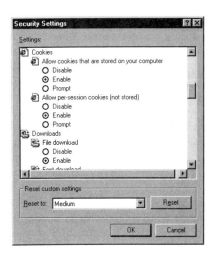

Changing security settings

2. Select Prompt in the Allow Cookies section, leave Enable selected in the Allow Per-Session Cookies section, and click OK.

3. Click Yes to confirm the change and then click OK to close the Internet Options dialog box.

4. To test the new setting, type *www.wired.com* in the Address bar and press Enter. You see this security alert:

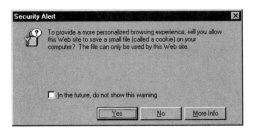

5. Click Yes or No, depending on your preference.

6. After viewing the online version of *Wired* magazine, click the Home button to return to familiar territory.

If you click No, some Web sites will allow you to view their pages but will try resending their cookies periodically. Some sites won't allow you to view their pages at all until you accept their cookies. If you get tired of dealing with the Security Alert dialog box, you can return to the Security Settings dialog box and set the Allow Cookies option to Enable.

Securing the System with Security Zones

Another area of security you may be concerned about is protecting your computer from the malignant viruses that can be introduced purposely or accidentally when you download files or run programs across the Internet. Internet Explorer fights contagion with a system of security zones that enable you to identify the sites you trust to send files to your computer and those you don't. Internet Explorer comes with four predefined security zones to which you can assign specific sites. You can then set the security level for each zone to reflect the extent to which you trust the assigned sites. Try this:

Where are cookies stored?

The cookies files are stored in a subfolder of the Windows folder called (surprise!) *Cookies*. If you are interested, you can use Windows Explorer to find a cookie file with today's date, right-click it, and choose Quick View from the shortcut menu to see what it looks like.

1. Choose Internet Options from the Tools menu and click the Security tab to display these options:

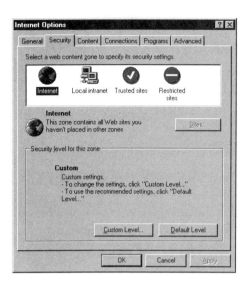

2. Click the Default Level button to restore the default security level to the selected zone (the Internet zone). This default security level is Medium, meaning that you will be warned before potentially damaging files are downloaded from sites in this zone (including the programs that make pictures and text on a Web page move). The Sites button is not available for this zone, because all sites not assigned to the other three zones are automatically members of the Internet zone.

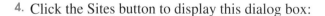
Internet zone

3. Select Trusted Sites in the Select A Web Content Zone box. This default security level is Low, meaning that you will not be warned about files downloaded from sites in this zone.

Trusted sites zone

4. Click the Sites button to display this dialog box:

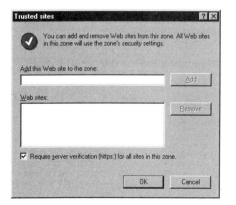

Cached sites are presumed safe

So that you won't be constantly interrupted by the Security Alert message box, the sites already cached on your computer are assumed by Internet Explorer to be safe, and minimal security settings are applied to them.

Be careful about which sites you add to the Trusted Sites zone, because you can never be totally sure about the files you are downloading. Also bear in mind that your company may have rules about which sites can be assigned to this zone.

5. Type *https://www.microsoft.com* in the Add This Web Site To The Zone edit box, click Add, and then click OK.

Restricted Sites zone

6. Now select Restricted Sites in the Select A Web Content Zone box. This default security level is High, meaning that files that could potentially damage your computer will not be downloaded from sites in this zone.

7. Click OK to close the dialog box without adding any sites to the Restricted Sites zone.

The zone to which the active Web site belongs appears at the right end of Internet Explorer's status bar at the bottom of the screen. When the program window is displayed in full-screen view, as it is now, you might want to turn on the status bar by choosing its command from the View menu. Then you can tell at a glance whether the site can be trusted enough to download files from it.

Certificates

Certificates are used primarily by secure sites that want to do business over the Internet. They are issued by independent organizations and they are date-stamped. Internet Explorer checks that the certificate is valid and current before downloading information from the site. If a site has no certificate, if the certificate's URL is different from the site's, or if the certificate has expired, Internet Explorer alerts you. You then decide whether to do business with the site. You can also use a personal certificate, also known as a *digital ID*.

Profile Assistant and Microsoft Wallet

Some Web sites require that you supply information about yourself before you can view them. Others require that you transmit address and payment information in order to make online purchases. To simplify the process of supplying this information, you can use the Profile Assistant to store and encrypt personal details and Microsoft Wallet to transmit credit card information without fear of it being purloined in transit. Web sites designed to work with both Profile Assistant and Microsoft Wallet can then request the information in a secure form from these programs, and you can approve or deny the request. (You will still have to deal manually with sites that are not set up to work with these "helpers.") To set up Profile Assistant, choose Internet Options from the Tools menu and click the Content tab. Then click My Profile in the Personal Information section to view and edit the information used by Profile Assistant. To set up Microsoft Wallet, simply click the Wallet button on the same tab of the same dialog box.

Censoring Web-Site Content

If you work or go to school in a big city, you know that if you take a certain route to get to work or school, you'll have to turn a blind eye to some of the unsavory characters and establishments you might see along the way. Even if you are prepared to handle the experience in the interest of getting from point A to point B as quickly as possible, you might not want your kid sister or brother wandering around in that neighborhood. The Internet is like a huge city, with all its diversity, both positive and negative. If you want to ensure that you never see potentially objectionable sites, you can turn to Content Advisor, which blocks access to sites that may contain offensive material. Follow these steps to set up Content Advisor:

Content Advisor

1. Choose Internet Options from the Tools menu and then click the Content tab of the Internet Options dialog box.

2. Next click Enable in the Content Advisor section. You then see this dialog box:

Other censors

Several programs are available with more sophisticated censoring capabilities than those of the Content Advisor, which relies exclusively on ratings of Web content. For example, Cyber Patrol from The Learning Company uses ratings but also allows users to develop lists of sites they want to avoid. SurfWatch from Surf-Watch Software relies not on ratings but on a list of objectionable sites that it updates daily on its Web site. Other programs include Net Nanny, X-Stop, and CyberSitter. Filtering programs can be time-consuming to figure out and set up, and even the more sophisticated ones are not foolproof. Ongoing vigilance is necessary if you are determined to shield yourself or your family from objectionable material.

3. Set the level for each category by selecting it and moving its rating slider. If you don't want any offensive language, nudity, sex, or violence, leave the sliders for all the categories set at Level 0 (all the way to the left).

4. When you are finished setting the content levels, click OK.

Now when anyone attempts to use your computer to display a Web site that is rated higher than the levels you set for language, nudity, sex, or violence, Internet Explorer blocks it. However, it's important to note that a great many Web sites don't yet have content ratings and that the technology is not totally foolproof. Obviously, sites with material that many people would deem offensive aren't going to seek a rating if the rating's only function is to provide a mechanism for blocking the site. By default, Content Advisor blocks all unrated sites once it is enabled, so it blocks thousands of perfectly innocent sites as well as the seedy ones. On the General tab of the Content Advisor dialog box, you can select an option to allow the display of unrated sites, but then you leave the gate open for the sites that are really offensive. Only you can decide on the best balance between information availability and protection.

You are now equipped to take advantage of all the Internet has to offer, both for work and play. Later, you may want to explore the many other ways you can customize Internet Explorer to meet your needs, whether for targeted research or random surfing. Have fun!

Index

See clearly—
now!

Here's the remarkable, *visual* way to quickly find answers about the powerfully integrated features of the Microsoft® Office 2000 applications. Microsoft Press AT A GLANCE books let you focus on particular tasks and show you, with clear, numbered steps, the easiest way to get them done right now. Put Office 2000 to work today, with AT A GLANCE learning solutions, made by Microsoft.

- MICROSOFT OFFICE 2000 PROFESSIONAL AT A GLANCE
- MICROSOFT WORD 2000 AT A GLANCE
- MICROSOFT EXCEL 2000 AT A GLANCE
- MICROSOFT POWERPOINT® 2000 AT A GLANCE
- MICROSOFT ACCESS 2000 AT A GLANCE
- MICROSOFT FRONTPAGE® 2000 AT A GLANCE
- MICROSOFT PUBLISHER 2000 AT A GLANCE
- MICROSOFT OFFICE 2000 SMALL BUSINESS AT A GLANCE
- MICROSOFT PHOTODRAW® 2000 AT A GLANCE
- MICROSOFT INTERNET EXPLORER 5 AT A GLANCE
- MICROSOFT OUTLOOK® 2000 AT A GLANCE

mspress.microsoft.com

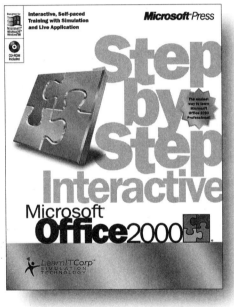